Engaged & Disengaged

Engaged & Disengaged

Douglas Bush

Harvard University Press
Cambridge, Massachusetts
1966

Distributed in Great Britain by Oxford University Press, London

Publication of this volume has been aided by a grant from the Hyder Edward Rollins Fund

Library of Congress Catalog Card Number 66–23462

Printed in the United States of America

To my colleagues of the Department of English
and the Director of Harvard University Press
whose friendship engendered this miscellany
and to a host of old students

Although conceived and sponsored by his colleagues at Harvard as a token of their great affection and esteem for Douglas Bush, this book can hardly be regarded as an act of homage because the honoré did all the work. None the less, we think that our benign intention was not entirely foiled, for in their wit and wisdom and felicity these essays do celebrate a good man and an illustrious career. In ways unknown to him, the author is the hero of this book.

H. B.

Contents

I

II

III

Contents

I

Memoirs of a Virtuous Family

To HAVE ENRICHED the English language with a word, and that word one's own name, is to have won the surest kind of immortality. Reputations based on mere artistic achievement "go up and down" as disconcertingly as Mr. Weller's "funs" did in the City, but when one has got oneself into the dictionary, into popular speech, even, it may be, into newspaper editorials, one is raised forever above the whims of movements and coteries. The name which inspired these solemn reflections is one that will live as long as Shakespeare's, perhaps longer. It is that of Bowdler.

The Bowdler pedigree deserves the attention of sociologists, as a sort of pendant to the unhappily famous Jukeses. The chronicle of various members of the family all leads up, as it were, to the glorious apotheosis of the best-known bearer of the name. One sees the genealogical tree putting forth here and there little tender shoots of Anglican piety and moral elevation and genteel culture and literary feeling, and, after a period of such quiet growth, gathering its sweetness into a ball — for one metaphor is inadequate — and giving to the world the editor of *The Family Shakespeare*. The *Memoir* is not, one may suspect, very widely read, and I shall quote without stint, for it has, in substance and style, a pervading flavor of its own. It was written by Thomas Bowdler, divine, eldest son of John Bowd-

Reprinted from *Life and Letters*, February 1929.

ler and nephew of the great Thomas. The title page runs: "Memoir of the late John Bowdler, Esq., to which is added Some Account of the late Thomas Bowdler, Esq., Editor of *The Family Shakespeare*. 'Trust in the Lord, and do good.' London. 1825."

We hardly need to be told that so far back as history extends the Bowdlers were "strictly upright, pious, and benevolent, maintaining sound principles both in Church and State." A Bowdler who went to Ireland as an official married a bishop's daughter, acquired a competence ("His name be praised!"), and died as he had lived, "bending heavenward all along." His infant son Thomas, who at three months had "a promise of blessing from heaven in his very countenance," was taken by an uncle in England, in accordance with the bishop's prayer that he be brought up in the Church of England and "kept from seedes of schisme and phanaticisme." The heavenly light in Thomas' countenance was by no means a false dawn. The youth showed himself "correct in his conduct . . . piously resigned in tribulation, perfectly acquainted with all matters of business," and it was doubtless this last qualification, if not the first, which recommended him to a post in the Admiralty, "next in situation to the learned and excellent Secretary Pepys."

Having retired from work rather early, in spite of some brotherly surprise on that score, Thomas died in 1738. He had occupied himself in various beneficent ways, and had enjoyed the friendship of Dr. Hickes, the Scandinavian scholar, and Sir Robert Cotton and his son. His son Thomas also abandoned business before his prime to taste the fruits of virtuous retirement at Bath. Even in his lifetime he was the subject of a public eulogy, which was the more sincere for being measured; a Bath publication pronounced him to be "one of the most benevolent men of that, or perhaps, any other place." His wife, as became a Cotton, had a distinctly literary turn. She was not only gentle, cultivated, devout, but must have possessed a singularly lucid mind, for to instruct her children "she drew up an explanation of the Church catechism, so comprehensive and yet so plain, that there is scarce any point of doctrine or duty, or of the discipline of our Church, which may not be learned from it."

"Thus trained in the good and right way . . . the son of these excellent parents acquired a knowledge of religion beyond his years, and firm principles of action, which gave him, while yet a boy, the fixed and steady character of a man." This admirable son was John Bowdler, the chief subject of the *Memoir*. He grew rapidly in grace and virtue. The inspiration afforded by the record of pious ancestry was already making itself felt, for John "himself expressed very feelingly his thankfulness for the good advice which he had received from his father, and his dread of falling into temptation, and being the first bad man of the family."

In 1765 he began to read law in the Temple. In that London of Selwyn and Wilkes, John Bowdler, happy with a few choice friends, continued in the exercise of rational virtue. "Mr. Bowdler at this time frequently attended the 'well-trod stage,'" but he later doubted if it could ever be "lawful for a Christian to seek his pleasure there, or to give countenance to anything so seductive and dangerous." The young man's principles were, of course, fortified by parental letters and exhortations, but these must be passed over. Nor can Mrs. Bowdler's writings be mentioned, except one treatise which contains "among other things, some very sensible observations on the question whether our Lord ate the Paschal Lamb on the night before he suffered, and some rules for forming a scheme of Scripture Chronology." Mrs. Bowdler's religion was "cheerful, and free from enthusiasm."

John continued to live in London, applying himself, also without enthusiasm, to the Law. In 1784 his eldest sister died. Her collected poems and essays reached a seventeenth edition by 1830 — which helps to explain popular neglect of Shelley and Keats. Her writings include an "Ode to Hope," "On the Death of Mr. Garrick" (in which are contrasted the favor of the pit and the favor of God), essays on such Bowdlerian topics as "Fortitude," "Resignation," "The Pleasures of Religion." The death of his father enabled John Bowdler to relinquish the Law and set up as a country gentleman. The extraordinary sensitiveness of his conscience may be judged from the fact that "his early knowledge of the Law made him a little fearful of acting as a magistrate," a scruple which must have been unique among eighteenth-century justices of the peace. An even greater delicacy prevented his accepting the office of churchwarden.

But in a larger sphere Mr. Bowdler was indefatigably benevolent. With his eye, like Burke's, on the French Revolution, he wrote a pamphlet, *Reform or Ruin.* In this plea for individual righteousness he first holds up for emulation the royal example of virtue and sobriety, and "afterwards addresses himself to those on whom Providence has bestowed rank, or honour, or wealth, or any other useful talent." From which one perceives that sound principles in Church and State were still a family inheritance. Bowdler denounced the profanation of the Lord's Day by newspapers and stagecoaches, and he urged the suppression of lotteries with an unexpectedly detailed knowledge of their fraudulent devices. He helped to raise a fund for the relief of that "very interesting portion of Christ's Church," the Episcopal Church of Scotland. One can give only a partial list of the many channels of Mr. Bowdler's moral energy — the S.P.C.K., the Society for the Suppression of Vice, the building of churches for that very interesting portion of God's handiwork, the middle and lower classes. He published poems, divine and moral. Indeed, "poetry had been at all times his delight," and he was constantly quoting "Shakespeare and Young." But though liberal he was never lax. "My dear Madam," he wrote, "I beg leave to return your book, for I cannot approve it. The author is plainly a Scotsman, and probably an Unitarian . . . ." In religion, as one would surmise, Bowdler "had much of feeling, but no enthusiasm." "It is better," he used to say, "to decide wrong than not to decide at all" — the motto, surely, of all successful moral reformers.

In 1799 a daughter died; "she drew a little, and that little was very elegant." In 1815 a son died. Heaven welcomed many Bowdlers at an early age. As for this son, better than the abundant testimony of others is his own exhortation to a schoolfellow: "Permit me to recommend *the strictest temperance*, which is equally indispensable, whether you wish to promote health, ability, happiness, or virtue. . . ." In his twentieth year he commenced an essay on the duties and advantages of affliction, a perennial theme among the much-enduring Bowdlers.

We have been slow in reaching Thomas Bowdler, but now he really needs no description; he was simply the sum, the fine flower, of the Bowdler virtues. As a child he won the love of relatives and the admiration of strangers. After taking a medical degree at Edinburgh in 1776 he carried about the Continent the judicial mind and incorruptible soul of his house. Abandoning his profession on his father's death, he became a Fellow of the Royal and Antiquarian Societies, and an ornament of Mrs. Montagu's sprightly but decorous circle. But a Bowdler could not remain a mere hanger-on of bluestockings, however decorous. Thomas "had imbibed an hereditary desire to be doing good; and happily the metropolis affords abundant opportunities of exercising benevolence." Like John, he was active in suppressing profane and immoral books. His minor writings must be passed by, to come to the great achievement of his life. "A literary object . . . undertaken chiefly with a view to the moral improvement of society, now engaged Mr. T. Bowdler's attention. This was no less than presenting the plays of Shakespeare to the public, purified from everything that could offend the most delicate eye or ear." And so there appeared "*The Family Shakespeare*. In ten Volumes, in which nothing is added to the original text, but those words and expressions are omitted which cannot with propriety be read aloud in a family. By Thomas Bowdler, Esq., F.R.S. and S.A."

While recognizing that Shakespeare's lapses in both profanity and indecency were due to the taste of the age as well as to "his own unbridled fancy," Bowdler was not the less strict in removing them. "The most Sacred Word in our language is omitted in a great number of instances, in which it appeared as a mere expletive; and it is changed to the word Heaven, in a still greater number, where the occasion of using it did not appear sufficiently serious to justify its employment." One cannot pass over the classic statement of his aims. "It certainly has been my wish, and it has been my study, to exclude from this publication whatever is unfit to be read aloud by a gentleman to a company of ladies. I can hardly imagine a more pleasing occupation for a winter's evening in the country, than for a father to read one of Shakespeare's plays to his family circle. My object is to enable him to do so without incurring the danger of falling unawares among words and expressions which are of such a nature as to raise a blush on the cheek of modesty, or render it necessary for the reader to pause, and examine the sequel, before he proceeds further in the entertainment of the evening." But Bowdler's delicate literary conscience would not permit him to make additions to the text beyond a few connecting particles. "I know the force of Shakespeare." he says, "and the weakness of my own pen, too well, to think of attempting the smallest interpolation," although "a word that is less objectionable is sometimes substituted for a synonymous word that is improper."

Shakespeare being rendered innocuous to modesty, the editor proceeded to a similar work "which he deemed of yet greater importance . . . a task well worthy of a man of sound principles and correct judgement," namely, the purification of Gibbon. "To this work Mr. T. Bowdler devoted much and diligent attention, and as his seventieth year drew on and infirmities increased, he made it his earnest prayer that he might be permitted to finish the important undertaking. This desire was granted."

One must resist the temptation to quote examples of Bowdler's revamping of Shakespeare and Gibbon. The biographer rejoices in the incontrovertible testimony to the merit of *The Family Shakespeare* afforded by its great and increasing sale. It "will be the edition which will lie on the table of every drawing-room; and the name of the editor will be remembered as one who has perhaps contributed more than any other individual to promote the innocent and rational amusement of well-educated families." However quaint a figure Thomas Bowdler is to us —

robed in snowy white, with the expurgated Shakespeare in one hand and the purified Gibbon in the other, shining forth, a beacon of rational virtue, in that wicked world of the Regency and His Christian Majesty George the Fourth — however quaint he may be, his nephew's eulogy proved, for several generations, to be absolutely true. And perhaps he did not irreparably cramp artistic freedom. One recalls, for instance, the picture of that insatiable little red-haired reader clutching his well-worn Bowdler in the hand that was to write *Laus Veneris* and *Anactoria*. And one wonders how such a dauntless soul as Bowdler would confront contemporary literature; would even his energetic scissors falter in the task of preparing a hearth-and-home edition of *Ulysses*? In our day, when calling a spade a spade — or a symbol — is frequently regarded as the height of imaginative creation, Bowdler seems as much a part of the dead past as a dinosaur. Yet he deserved at least as well of Shakespeare as, say, Mr. Frank Harris, and if nothing more he should be cherished in memory as a highly significant fossil. It was soon after he died that the Young Girl rose in her majestic innocence and was officially recognized as the tenth and presiding muse of the next literary era, and, if chronology and morality permitted, it might be affirmed that she was the perfectly natural daughter of the Princess Victoria and Thomas Bowdler, Esq., F.R.S. and S.A.

An Apologie for the Scepticall Reader:

Consisting in an Examination and Censure of the Common Errour Touching Natures Decay and the Complexity and Corruption of the World in these Late Times

The worshipful young gentleman that ruleth over this Society, accosting me some weeks since — it was, if I mistake not, the anniversary day whereon his Majesty and the two Houses of Parliament were delivered from the diabolical Powder Plot — the young gentleman entreated me, in the wantonness of his humor, to attend at this banquet and discourse somewhat thereafter of virtue and good letters. I recall not the exact words of his speech, wherein it may be he did not touch virtue, yet no judicious mind could doubt of his intention. At the first hearing, or, as Tully hath it, on being propositioned, I stood a while irresolute. Taking counsel with myself, I was unwilling that so great a cause should suffer injury from one so wanting in wisdom and eloquence as I knew myself to be. I had regard to the withered and sapless condition whereto much study and

A speech given at the Christmas dinner of the Signet Society, Cambridge, Massachusetts, December 1, 1954.

crabbed age, *tetrica senectus*, have brought me. I had regard likewise to the jovial and fiery spirits that would, I foresaw, be dancing about this board, both in cups and in mercurial wits. A leaden-eyed scholar, born under Saturn, how should he go about to tickle the ears of young hopeful imps of Apollo? Moreover, I said to myself, will brisk juvenals be eager to climb, or even to look upon, the steep, rugged hill of virtue and poesy when all are weighted, *pleno ventre*, with full belly, by the gifts of Ceres and Bacchus?

Notwithstanding the queasy stomach wherewith I contemplated this adventure, it yet seemed a scurvy thing to draw back, both because of the honor bestowed in the asking and because of the good will I have toward the gentlemen of this choice Society and toward all who either augment or cherish the rich treasures of man's invention. For, had we not those treasures, we should be as oxen in the field, apprehending no higher conceit than this cow and this grass, and choking with rude ignorance and blindness the ethereal spark that burns in man's soul. Surely, then, it behooves us on all fit occasions to bear witness to the noble office of the poet, by which title I intend no vulgar distinction between verse and prose but all true and sound works that are born of man's Promethean faculty and are formed by discreet judgment.

Many men complain that poetry is not now held in that honor and estimation she was. In all former ages, say they, wherein any light of learning and civility shined, poetry was reputed a divine skill. As Master Benjamin Jonson, that diligent ornament of this age, hath stoutly declared, the poet comes forth the interpreter and arbiter of nature, a teacher of things divine no less than human, a master in manners. So it was in Greece and Rome: so it has been more lately in Italy, France, England, and other nations.

Yet now, say these men, in the mere short course of their own lifetime, the honor of poesy has decayed and become a mark for railing rhetoric, and this for several manifest reasons. One is the springing up of divers new knowledges that, Gorgon-like, turn poetry to stone, or rather, like the Chimaera, shrivel it into ashes with scorching breath. Moreover, under the cover of these new knowledges, the fat-witted multitude, always agog for some new garment wherewith to hide their nakedness, and knowing naught of the sweetness and majesty of poetry, stick foul reproaches upon her. Of what use is a poet, they say, scoffing; why are poets poor, but that they are too simple to grow rich?

The chief of these new enemies of poetry and true learning are that sect of restless inquiring heads that pursue natural philosophy. One noted philosopher of pregnant parts has affirmed that "The use of this feigned history" — by which he signifieth poetry — "hath been to give some shadow of satisfaction to the mind of man in those points wherein the nature of things doth deny it, the world being in proportion inferior to the soul: by reason whereof there is, agreeable to the spirit of man, a more ample greatness, a more exact goodness, and a more absolute variety, than can be found in the nature of things." Hence poetry hath the sovereign power to reward virtue and to punish vice, whereas history, as was remarked of the illustrious Sir Philip Sidney, is captived to the truth of a foolish world and must set forth the issues of actions as they happed, without regard to good or evil. So, better than history, poetry serves magnanimity, morality, and delectation. But although the philosopher thus praises poetry in that it exalts the spirit of man, on the other hand he censures it as not obedient to truth, and this he doth the more strongly because he busies himself especially with exact searching into natural causes and effects, seeking thereby to establish man's power over nature. He concludes accordingly that poesy submits the shows of things to the desires of the mind, whereas reason doth buckle and bow the mind unto the nature of things. To the same effect he sayeth that it is not good to stay too long in the theatre, inferring that which the poet or maker invents to be no more real than a stage spectacle.

Set over against the dry light of reason and the truth of nature, poetry, if we heed such opinions, shrinks into a toy, a mere phantasma, a kind of pleasurable deceit whereby we are persuaded to view man and man's life as better and nobler than they are. Thus is poesy haled before the bar of truth and proclaimed a liar, because those things only are true that can be measured with a tailor's yard. There are indeed nurseries where this poor sort of knowledge is cultivated with much zeal, and that yield plentiful crops of sow-thistles and brambles, as pragmatical wits have learned of their great master-gardener, one John Dee or Dewey.

So diverse are the motions of man's thought in this late and unsettled age of the world, there be others that esteem poetry a kind of truth and no toy, but yet would have poets show forth the utter vanity and wretchedness of man as being helpless to raise himself out of the mire of misfortune and iniquity in which he is born and lives out his life. This doctrine also can call natural philosophy its father, because some authors — we will not call them poets — have maintained that they must tread close in the steps of the natural philosophers and write only those things concerning man and man's life that can be, as their word is, verified. Our academic scholars, those whose heads have been turned by the new empirical philosophy, hold that such authors trace in man's thought and actions the working of what they misname the laws of nature, taking no account of good and evil as distinguished by the true laws of nature, whereof Cicero and the Stoics have written.

Some men, too, that otherwise have inclined to think nobly of man, while yet acknowledging the weakness of his reason and the unruly force of his will, have been rendered deject and spiritless when they considered the unceasing discords and wars that make up the sum of history, as we read in the book of Sir Walter Ralegh wherein he digesteth the records of the ancient Hebrews and Greeks and Romans. But that which most of all crusheth the spirit of this sort of men is the perceiving that in this respect man has grown rather worse than better, in those many ages that have passed since he received a higher vision of good than was vouchsafed to the ethnics. And whereas in old times men fought with spear and sword and the trusty long-bow, first the cross-bow, then that devilish engine of nitrous powder leveled all martial prowess and glory, making Thersites a match for Achilles. What monstrous instruments of war our posterity may contrive, we must not think. Indeed the world even now seems to have run mad, intent upon her own destruction. Tearful Peace, following the fair virgin Astraea, has betaken herself from the wicked earth to the skies. Thus speak many good men of clear judgment that do not use to be easily swayed.

Interrupting our grieffull argument for a space, methinks the writers of this critical and splenetic age too rarely make us laugh, albeit we have much need of laughter. Many good authors of former ages overflowed with jollity, such as Boccace, in his tales of lewd monks, and our esteemed poet Chaucer, who did not disdain to lower his courtly style to the scapes of carpenters and friars, or Rabelais with his giants Gargantua and Pantagruel and the merry quest of the Holy Bottle. Honest mirth is a cleanser and restorer of the soul; it purgeth many troubles and sickly vanities, especially in them that brood overmuch on themselves. Mirth indeed bringeth about, as Aristotle and the Italians might allow, a kind of catharsis, if so be that the author is a lover and not a despiser of man. For the highest reach of mirth does in some measure partake of sober sadness. In witness whereof are the lean and foolish knight of Cervantes, ever seeking to set right the manifold wrongs of the world, or those clowns of our Master Shakespeare — Sir John Falstaff, Bully Bottom, and the like, that are happy in their wit or in their witlessness. In such persons, as well as in the princes and nobles of stately tragedy, a mirror is held up to nature and we see therein somewhat of ourselves; our pride is humbled and we feel as brothers of all mankind.

Returning to our former discourse, there is another set of melancholy men that talk after this manner: "What though there were no war or rumors of war, life in these times is not what it was. Nature and men are alike decayed. King James is no Queen Elizabeth; the ruler of this great nation ofttimes leaveth his weighty business and spendeth many days together in sport. Of high and low, few there be that are not possessed by the love of having, *amor habendi*, as Naso calleth it. Sir Giles Mompesson, that has heaped up much wealth by the licensing of inns and other monopolies, doth not stick to aver that what is good for monopolies is good for the nation. Greed and fraud thrive apace; honest men go bare. The Gospel is taught, not learned. Charity is key-cold. The young scorn old ways and mock their reverend fathers. Every day brings forth fresh, span-new opinions. More and more gentlemen exhaust their purses with indulgence in that precious stink, tobacco. Not alone base mechanicals but sleek mercers and vintners clap their fat hands when a knavish orator flatters their ignorance and bids them beware of the traitorous Anabaptists." So do many men speak of the good old times, and of the scrofulous and scabby present. Our time, say they, hath not seen the like of Sir Philip Sidney; it was not men of our debased breed that scattered the Armada in the glorious year eighty-eight.

And no less woeful are these malcontents when they look asquint at the state of letters and see all things changed for the worse. Little children spell out foolish stories in foolish pictures. Their elders, they that read anything, have a taste for naught but romances of Guy of Warwick and Bevis of Hampton, or the news of horrid murders vended by pedlars. Scarce a cat can look out of a gutter but out starts a halfpenny chronicler, and presently a proper new ballad of a strange sight is indited. There is a swarm of poetasters, bearded like the pard, that write huffing satires, mouthing rough words out of Juvenal and Persius — for, they affirm, the vices of old Rome were not worse than those of London. In our fathers' time the best poets taught old and young to love beauty and goodness, in verse smooth and rich as cream. The admired Spenser saw corruptness all about him; notwithstanding, he built a stately house of heroic virtues, which all could enter and behold how great and good men might be. Our best poet now, men say, is the Dean of St. Paul's, who, for all his years and holy office, has not left off versing. As a young man upon the town Dr. Donne was given to loose conversation, yet had withal deep learning and a high and ingenious capacity, and every ink-squittering springald that craved reputation must needs take Jack Donne for his model. But the witty gallant shifted his amorousness from women to heaven, whither not many were ready to follow him. It was Jack Donne that first made poetry rough and difficult to be understood; only strong lines were in request and approved. Wherefore the only persons that now read poetry are poets, or else those fastidious Inns of Court men that have appointed themselves to sit as Minoses on the life and death of works. They loll in taverns over their sack and, as they say, "explicate" poems to each other; for they delight in ink-horn terms wherewith to astound the vulgar. After the fifth cup they will tell you that all ages were happy up till this present, but that now is the age of anxiety, wherein miserable man can do naught but cling to despair.

Of these new topsy-turvy ways I myself know but little. I report only what things I have collected from the young, in part from the son of my kinsman, Justice Shallow. This man, Thomas by name, had in his youth no proper respect for his father, which indeed is not hard to understand, and applied his mind wholly to poets and poetry. Hence when he should have been conning his law books he haunted the taverns with the hope to gape at, or even speak with, some of our famous writers and players. It so happened once that Thomas, after many hours wasted in such busy idleness, had a singular piece of good fortune. First he fell in with some spruce critical wits that he had noted at Clement's Inn and he listened to their talk. Some berated Shakespeare roundly for being of the old fashion, mocking the high heroic love of Romeo and Juliet: what is love, said they, but the sport of venery? Here one named *Troilus and Cressida*, urging that this comical satire was indeed a true mirror of war and lechery. So much the others grudgingly allowed, yet they would have none of *Hamlet*, *King Lear*, and *Macbeth*: "We have outgrown those old simple notions of good and evil, we be of the age of confusion."

Master Thomas, a well-disposed lad, not overliking such saucy railing, slipped away to the Mermaid tavern, where, his mind still aflutter, he sat him down on a bench near two men that were deep in talk and drink. They spoke much of the Globe and the Blackfriars and of masques at the court, and now and then called each other by name, as Ben and Will, whereat it came upon young Thomas that these two could be no other than the renowned Ben Jonson and the worthy Will Shakespeare. After his ears had drunk in what they could, Thomas at length resolved to speak, albeit astonished at his own forwardness. "Master Shakespeare," said he, somewhat haltingly, as both turned their eyes upon him, "I am the son of Justice Shallow, whom you know. I have lately come from a company where there was a deal of new-fangled talk, and where you were berated for following old simple notions of love and good and evil, such as our grandsires held. Good Master Shakespeare, is this present the age of anxiety? Tell me, I pray, art thou confused?"

Whereupon, as Thomas hath narrated a score of times, the burly Jonson threw himself back on the bench, exclaiming, with a loud hiccup, "An arrant fool, a simpleton, as brainless as one of his father's Cotswold sheep!" But Master Shakespeare only smiled upon him and said, or rather sung softly:

When that I was and a little tiny boy,
  With hey, ho, the wind and the rain,
A foolish thing was but a toy,
  For the rain it raineth every day. . . .

A great while ago the world begun,
  With hey, ho, the wind and the rain,
But that's all one, our play is done,
  And we'll strive to please you every day.

Mrs. Bennet and the Dark Gods: The Key to Jane Austen

Although our age has witnessed the superseding of tame traditional criticism by the anthropological-psychological method, the study of Jane Austen has not yet caught up with the new movement. Her critics still talk about "social comedy" and "eighteenth-century rationality" and the like. The revolutionary exponents of archetypal myth, who have revealed unsuspected depths in many familiar works of literature, have quite failed to see Jane Austen's essential affinity with Melville and Kafka.

That her mythic patterns should have gone so long unrecognized is startling evidence of the real subtlety of her mind and art, which have been so much praised for shallow reasons. Even a brief examination of the occult structuring of *Pride and Prejudice* will establish Jane Austen's claim to be the first great exemplar of the modern mythic consciousness. If conventional criticism should object that she was a notably rational person, and that she had read little outside eighteenth-century belles lettres, it may be said in reply that it is of the essence of the mythic technique that it should be at least half unconscious, that its operations should disclose themselves only to the anthropological critic. It may be granted that the various myths which

Reprinted by permission from *The Sewanee Review*, October 1956.

underlie the smooth and simple surface of *Pride and Prejudice* are not fully and organically developed but — in keeping with the fragmentariness of the modern psyche and its world — are only momentarily touched or blended in nebulous and shifting configurations; yet their presence in depth re-creates the values implicit in the outwardly commonplace situations of genteel village life. In mythic criticism the great thing is to find some semi-submerged rocks to stand on.

To the average casual reader, the first short chapter of *Pride and Prejudice* appears only to state the common theme of love and marriage, to set forth the character and situation of Mr. and Mrs. Bennet and their five marriageable daughters, and to report the arrival in the neighborhood of a highly eligible young bachelor, Mr. Bingley. Yet, from this brief and supposedly comic exposition, hints of the mythic and even mystic emerge. The famous first sentence, "It is a truth universally acknowledged, that a single man in possession of a good fortune must be in want of a wife," goes far beyond surface literalness. For on the next page we are told that Mrs. Bennet had been a beauty, and the single man in want of a wife reflects that desire for perpetuation of beauty expounded in Plato's *Symposium*. Ironically, although Mrs. Bennet has, in Platonic language, experienced "birth in beauty" five times, only one of her daughters is really beautiful; but it is this one that soon attracts Bingley.

Further, who and what is Bingley, the mysterious, ebullient stranger from the north who descends with his band of followers (his two sisters and Mr. Hurst and Mr. Darcy) upon a sleepy, conventional society and whom young people at once look to for providing dances? Clearly he is Dionysus, the disturbing visitor from northern Thrace.

And who then is Pentheus, the king of Thebes who resisted the newcomer and was torn to pieces by the Maenads led by his own mother? Such violent data had to be somewhat adjusted by the author, yet it is hardly less clear that Pentheus is Mr. Bennet, the king of his small domain who is resentful of strangers and professedly unwilling to call on Bingley (his lack of tragic integrity is betrayed by his actually calling), and who undergoes a symbolic death in that he has no son and that his estate is entailed. Mrs. Bennet, to be sure, is not responsible for the entail, but she nags about it constantly, and she has urged her husband to cultivate Bingley, so that she must be a surrogate for Pentheus' Maenad mother. Bingley's fortune is a patent transliteration of the ivy and wine of Dionysus (the family money had been acquired in trade, undoubtedly distilling); and his sudden, unexplained comings and goings correspond to the epiphanies of the god. The mythic character of Darcy and of his relation to Bingley is less certain. However, his dominating personality and his initial blindness to the charms of Elizabeth Bennet suggest the blind seer Tiresias as the mentor of Dionysus-Bingley. (I pass by the obvious homosexuality; on this level the two men are Hercules and Hylas.) Thus the simple persons and incidents of the novel take on from the start richly evocative and even sinister connotations.

As the story proceeds and tensions develop, the mythic pattern, and with it some individual roles, undergo subtle transformations; one myth shades into another. The once pretty Mrs. Bennet, whose sole concern is to get her daughters married, is an embodiment of the unthinking life-force that works through women, and she is Dionysiac in her devotion to Bingley. Her motherhood and her earthy mentality might at first suggest identification with the Earth

Goddess, but one explicit clue indicates that she is the goddess of love, born of the sea — she is a native of Meryton, the town of *mare*, the sea. On this new level, Mr. Bennet is more complex and obscure, because in projecting him Miss Austen uses not so much the orthodox and familiar myth of Venus and Adonis but some Renaissance variations of it. On the one hand, in his cool indifference to his emotional wife and in his desire to be left alone in his library, Mr. Bennet is the cold Adonis, intent on his hunting, of Shakespeare's poem. On the other hand, Jane Austen fuses with this conception the Neoplatonic symbolism of Spenser's "Garden of Adonis": as an intellectual, and the parent of five daughters, Mr. Bennet is Spenser's Adonis, "the father of all Forms," and Mrs. Bennet is Spenser's Venus, simply unformed Matter. Whatever skepticism conventional scholarship may have concerning some of these interpretations, no one could dispute this last point.

But the security of Venus and Adonis is threatened (and will eventually be destroyed) by the Boar. In Jane Austen's multiple layers of meaning, the Boar is the entail, which comes into force with Mr. Bennet's death and which is personified in his heir, Rev. Mr. Collins. We have here what is perhaps the most striking mythic ambiguity in the book: Mr. Collins is both the Boar and the Bore (and his clerical status adds a further though unexploited element of traditional ritualism). Mr. Collins is in fact the axis of several polarities.

As if this interweaving of mythic patterns were not complex enough, the same pattern, with new features added, is worked out on another level and takes shape as the central figure in the carpet. The older Venus and Adonis are partly paralleled in a younger Venus and Adonis, Elizabeth and the initially proud and indifferent Darcy; but this second version operates in a vein of paradox. Mr. Bennet had in his youth been allured by a pretty face and had later discovered the stupidity behind it; Darcy, at first cold and then attracted by beauty, discovers the spirit and charm that go with it and falls deeply in love. Elizabeth, though misled for a time by the specious Wickham (a sort of Anteros), comes to love Darcy in her turn. But the security of the young pair's new relation is threatened by a variety of circumstances and most explicitly by a new Boar-Bore, not now Mr. Collins but his patroness, Lady Catherine (who has also some Gorgonish traits). Mr. Collins, like the mythical boar, while really killing had only sought to kiss (he proposed to Elizabeth); Lady Catherine, seeking to kill the relation between her nephew Darcy and Elizabeth, instead brings about his renewed proposal and acceptance. Some of these features of the design have, it is true, been noticed in conventional criticism, but only on the personal and social level; the deeper dimensions and reverberations have been completely missed.

There are many particulars one would like to go into, for instance, Elizabeth's uncle, Mr. Gardiner, whom Darcy so unexpectedly invites to fish on his estate: what is Mr. Gardiner's relation to the Fisher King, and what of the veiled phallicism in the allusion to fishing tackle? [1] But only one other thread in the variegated web of complexity can be touched upon, the most central of all archetypal myths, the theme of death and rebirth. Jane Austen's heavy reliance upon this is all the more remarkable because she is commonly said to avoid the subject of death altogether; she never has a principal character die and only rarely reports

[1] When the results of this inquiry were first set forth, one very obvious point was overlooked — Mr. Gardiner's relation to the first gardener, Adam. It is unthinkable that Jane Austen should not have been concerned with the theme of all literature, the Fall.

such remote deaths as may contribute to the plot. But the real reason now becomes apparent: she did not deal with the subject in ordinary ways simply because her stories of young love are set against a dark mythic background of death. In *Pride and Prejudice* hints of mortality appear at the very beginning, in such place names as Longbourn ("man goeth to his long home"; "The undiscover'd country from whose bourn No traveller returns") and Netherfield (the nether or lower world). There is a recurrent stress on physical frailty: Kitty Bennet has spells of coughing; Jane Bennet falls ill at Netherfield; Anne de Bourgh is sickly; and there is a whole crowd of adults whose parents are dead; etc. We have already observed the insistent significance of the entail and Mr. Collins, who will inherit the estate when Mr. Bennet dies. In proposing to Elizabeth, the magnanimous Mr. Collins says that he knows she will, after her mother's death, have no more than a thousand pounds in the four per cents. Such hieroglyphics of pain and death, both mythic and worldly, are reinforced by the process of the seasons. The book opens in early autumn, and in this season of harvest and death there is the ritual dance, which, ominously, takes place at Netherfield, Bingley's house. It is during the late autumn and winter that blows fall upon the Bennets — Mr. Collins' unhappy visit, Bingley's departure and abandoning of Jane Bennet and her heavy disappointment and Elizabeth's sympathy for her. The worst blow, Lydia's elopement with Wickham (note, by the way, the ancient view of the shallow, sensual quality of Lydian music), does occur in the summer, but it is this event that sets everything in motion toward rebirth, or what is crudely called a happy ending. Darcy — now a saving Hercules — rescues Lydia and wins Elizabeth; Dionysus-Bingley returns and is restored to Jane; and Mrs.

Bennet, again a radiant Venus, rises from the depths in a foam of rejoicing.

Almost all the characters and incidents of the novel, under close scrutiny, will yield their mythic overtones, but perhaps enough has been said here to stimulate a critic who has the time and the insight for fuller investigation. The subject of archetypal myth in Jane Austen needs a book, and will doubtless get one.

A Note on Dickens' Humor

THE CHANGE IN THE CRITICAL view of Dickens during the past generation has been so marked that even the general reader could hardly miss it, and it has now been placed in its historical sequence in George H. Ford's scholarly and lively book, *Dickens and his Readers* (1955). Critics of older generations — both those who gladly surrendered to the magician's spell and those who remained austerely and somewhat snobbishly censorious — were likely to see an unsophisticated, erratic, inspired genius who gave his enormous public what it wanted: crude melodrama, crude pathos, and humanitarian zeal, a world of evil-doing and crime set off against the virtues, sorrows, and joys of the poor, a world of coaches and snug inns and cosy domesticity and good cheer, through which wandered characters of prodigious and eccentric vitality and humor.

The new Dickens has been seen (at least after the first frenzied phase of his career) as a highly conscious and developing artist, a sophisticated molder of symbolic patterns, a savage analyst of society, a half-surrealist creator of the crowded, lonely city, a novelist or novelist-poet to be read as we read Dostoevsky or Kafka or Faulkner. The

Reprinted from *From Jane Austen to Joseph Conrad: Essays Collected in Memory of James T. Hillhouse*, ed. Robert C. Rathburn and Martin Steinmann, Jr. (Minneapolis: University of Minnesota Press, 1958).

qualities of the old and the new Dickens cannot be summed up in two sentences, but these headings will serve. The new Dickens has become so well established, in the United States at any rate, that Mario Praz's hostile version of the old Dickens in his *The Hero in Eclipse* (1956) appears as something of an anachronism (like the present essay, except that this is not hostile). The change may be welcome even to those readers of the older or oldest generation who grew up on Dickens. The enchanter of children and of people in their second childhood, who used to invite critics' condescension, has now acquired an artistic stature commensurate with the enjoyment he has always given to the uncritical; what had seemed to be the beer of the populace was really 84-proof brandy. All this is much to the good, and we may hope for more analysis of the potencies and subtleties of Dickens' art.

At the same time it may be hoped that the new criticism of Dickens will not become too severely and solemnly intellectual and analytical. After all, as Mr. Sleary said, "People mutht be amuthed." Some modern critics give the impression of having come to Dickens late in life, perhaps after Dostoevsky, Kafka, and Faulkner (or perhaps after Stendhal, Flaubert, and James), and, however freshly illuminating, do not seem to be very much aware that Dickens is one of the world's greatest humorists — a fact not concealed from the most unexpected of Dickensians, Santayana. Dickens is, to be sure, many other things also, yet the millions who have rejoiced in his comic characters and dialogue may have been wiser than those children of light who either are unresponsive or regard humor as outside the critical pale.

These few pages are not a contribution to criticism; they are — in addition to being a small but cordial tribute to my old friend James Hillhouse (this piece was written before his illness and death) — only reminders of one rich element in some of the greatest comic characters we have. I am thinking of what may be loosely called the instinct for self-dramatization. Since Percy Lubbock's book, at least, it has been a commonplace that Dickens' novelistic technique is "dramatic" (as contrasted with Thackeray's "pictorial" narrative), but the author's dramatic handling of his material is not the same thing as the individual character's dramatizing of himself, though the two can come together. And, while Dickens' devotion to the stage — and the stagy — is a familiar fact, it does not alone explain the frequently theatrical quality of his comic characters' self-dramatization.

Not to refine overmuch, we might say that a character's humor may be unconscious and naive or conscious and — very probably — ironical, and that either attitude may have a touch of the histrionic. Such combinations are not of course peculiar to Dickens (or to English humor). Thus Chaucer's Miller is consciously giving himself a comic role when he declares, beginning with a high-flown phrase:

> But first I make a protestacioun
> That I am dronke, I knowe it by my soun.

So too when the Pardoner is called on for a tale and, his character being evident, the "gentils" cry out against ribaldry and demand "som moral thyng":

> "I graunte, ywis," quod he, "but I moot thynke
> Upon som honest thyng while that I drynke."

In these simple words the Pardoner suggests that he is capable, with a dubious stimulant, of telling a moral tale, even if it is not his line, that he is amused by the genteel pilgrims' anxiety, and that he enjoys keeping them in suspense.

The self-dramatizing instinct is obvious in Shakespeare's comic characters. The clowns, from the nature of their profession, are continually engaged in a sort of parody of the normal sanity, intelligence, and learning they are not supposed to possess. Falstaff, whether in the tavern or on the battlefield, is so consistently acting a part — the part of Falstaff — that whatever personality he may be imagined to have had has been absorbed into his conscious role. When he stages the little impromptu drama with Prince Hal and acts the part of the royal father and then of the son, he merely steps out of his everyday role into another of slightly heightened exaggeration. Falstaff not only acts in the presence of other people, the exalted as well as his Eastcheap cronies; he acts for the pure love of acting when he has no audience but himself, as in the delivery of his speech on honor.

Even the stiff and sober Malvolio has his high imaginings, when he is beguiled into seeing himself as Olivia's husband. He and the lowly Bottom both belong to the naive end of the spectrum; in both, self-dramatizing (which is instinctive and habitual with Bottom) is an unconscious revelation of vanity and stupidity — though one character is likable and the other is not. Neither has any protective irony, and each has a moment of unwitting self-deflation: Malvolio, in his vision of future greatness, stumbles into the thought of his still fingering his steward's chain (which he hastily amends to "some rich jewel"); and Bottom, waking after his experience with the ass's head, stops on the brink of admitting what he was and had. Yet each of the two has a measure of half-conscious artistry. Malvolio, in picturing his prospective elevation, speaks — for the delight of his own ear

— with a new degree of pomposity; and Bottom, likewise soliloquizing, seeks to do justice to his dream with a garbled version of I Corinthians 2.9: "The eye of man hath not heard, the ear of man hath not seen, man's hand is not able to taste, his tongue to conceive, nor his heart to report what my dream was." Perhaps the most consistent self-dramatizer is the drunken Stephano in *The Tempest.*

It is a question in which category, the naive or the conscious, to put Barnardine, the obstinate convict in *Measure for Measure*, who speaks only a few lines but is decidedly a personality. Is he displaying only crass obtuseness, or conscious humor, in the face of death? "Friar, not I! I have been drinking hard all night, and I will have more time to prepare me . . . I will not consent to die this day, that's certain . . . Not a word! If you have anything to say to me, come to my ward; for thence will not I to-day."

In exploiting the instinct for self-dramatization Dickens is very much in the tradition. This instinct is not only widespread among his comic characters; it may be their whole existence. These diverse and wonderful individuals have generally two things in common. First, they are very poor in this world's goods and live on the ragged edge, economically and socially; their lives, viewed objectively, are seedy and difficult enough to cause unrelieved depression or despair. Secondly, they have one supreme possession, an overflowing, irrepressible imagination, with its attendant gift of words, which transfigures themselves and their world, which makes their shabby existence a perpetual and exciting drama, and which no amount of painful experience can more than momentarily crush. In Dickens' vision, as in Blake's, all men — or a good many — are poets; and their speeches are the romantic poetry of Cockneydom. This faculty, at its best, seems to be both instinctive and half-conscious; its possessor is being himself and at the same time has a detached enjoyment of himself. Doubtless the psychologists have a word for it.

This mode of comprehension and creation was strong in Dickens from the beginning. Mr. Pickwick is not one of the self-dramatizers — his simplicity and innocence are too complete for that — but his fellow Pickwickians to some degree are, in assuming the roles of lover, poet, and sportsman which they cannot sustain. Jingle, the down-at-heel actor and adventurer, maintains a jaunty buoyancy through his own comic invention and resourcefulness; he is always presenting some other self to the world. Rachael Wardle sees herself as a romantic figure in her belated and short-lived love affairs. Even the fat boy is a conscious dramatic artist in working on the grandmother's feelings — "I wants to make your flesh creep." Sam Weller's self-dramatizing partakes largely of the knowingness of the smart Cockney. His father is a less slick and more primitive philosopher of man and matrimony, but he can also speak of himself with a mixture of complacency and detached irony (we are not quite sure where the division comes):

> "I'm a-goin' to leave you, Samivel, my boy, and there's no tellin' ven I shall see you again. Your mother-in-law may ha' been too much for me, or a thousand things may have happened by the time you next hears any news o' the celebrated Mr. Veller o' the Bell Savage. The family name depends wery much upon you, Samivel, and I hope you'll do wot's right by it. Upon all little pints o' breedin' I know I may trust you as vell as if it was my own self. . . ."

Even so might the bearer of an ancient and noble name counsel his heir.

There are endless varieties of comic fantasy, oblique wish-fulfillment. The members of the Crummles troupe support one another in their stagy affectations, which are their unconscious defense against the knowledge that they exist on the lowest level of the profession. The supreme dramatic imagination in this book, however, is Mrs. Nickleby's. In her it takes the form, not of humorous invention, but of naive reminiscence, since she instinctively evades the troubles of the present by living almost wholly, and blissfully, in the past. (One says "almost wholly" in the past because Mrs. Nickleby becomes, in her own imagination, the attractive heroine of a highly dramatic romance, her admirer being the lunatic next door who throws cucumbers over the wall.) Yet Mrs. Nickleby's flow of reminiscence (she is an early exemplar of the interior monologue) can hardly be called self-centered; rather, her past reflects a general rosy glow. And her recollections, if wayward, rarely lack dramatic particularity:

"Roast pig—let me see. On the day five weeks after you were christened we had a roast—no, that couldn't have been a pig either, because I recollect there were a pair of them to carve, and your poor papa and I could never have thought of sitting down to two pigs; they must have been partridges. Roast pig! I hardly think we ever could have had one, now I come to remember; for your papa could never bear the sight of them in the shops, and used to say that they always put him in mind of very little babies, only the pigs had much fairer complexions; and he had a horror of little babies, too, because he couldn't very well afford any increase to his family, and had a natural dislike to the subject . . ."

There are perhaps four self-dramatizers of superlative quality and consistency. The earliest of the quartet is Dick Swiveller. In his first appearance his taste for flamboyant rhetoric (which is often interlaced with scraps from popular songs) draws from his friend Fred the sour rebuke, "You needn't act the chairman here." But Dick acts at all times. And he is not only dramatic in himself but the cause that drama is in other men, as in the high quarrel with the rival suitor of Miss Wackles, whom Dick is trying to cast off ("Sorry, ma'am! . . . sorry in the possession of a Cheggs!"). He is lending himself to a sordid project, but what he does, or is willing to do, we forget in the joy of what he says. The scene between Dick and the Marchioness has long been recognized as one of the finest examples of Dickens' material and art, a unique blend of realism, romance, comedy, and sentiment that never approaches sentimentality. (If the pair could be imagined in a French novel, they would have a squalid liaison; in a Russian novel, Dick would be a revolutionist intellectual and the Marchioness a girl with a yellow ticket.) The scene in the basement kitchen is the great example of Dick's conscious, comic theatricalism (and goodness of heart):

> "Marchioness, your health. You will excuse my wearing my hat, but the palace is damp, and the marble floor is — if I may be allowed the expression — sloppy." . . .
>
> "Ha!" said Mr. Swiveller, with a portentous frown. " 'Tis well. Marchioness! — but no matter. Some wine there. Ho!" He illustrated these melodramatic morsels by handing the tankard to himself with great humility, receiving it haughtily, drinking from it thirstily, and smacking his lips fiercely.

By the way, to inject a bit of scholarship into this paper, is Dick's injunction to the Marchioness as she drinks the purl made from his own recipe — "moderate your transports" — an echo of Wordsworth's Protesilaus rebuking Laodamia, "thy transports moderate"?

In contrast with Mr. Swiveller's many roles, which range from the supposedly jealous lover to the theatrical bandit, the dirty, vulgar, callous, bibulous, and belligerent Mrs. Gamp might seem to be the husky voice of unadulterated nature. Yet the thought of Mrs. Gamp calls up at once that substantial product of her imagination, Mrs. Harris. Mrs. Harris might appear to prove the uniquely dramatic and disinterested creativity of Mrs. Gamp's mind if it were not that Mrs. Harris' chief function is to provide quotable encomiums on Mrs. Gamp. It is true that Mrs. Gamp's imagination is not quite completely circumscribed and self-centered — one of her most famous and breathless passages is the gratuitous account of Mr. Harris' anxieties over the birth of his first child — and Mrs. Harris is so real in her own mind that Mrs. Prig's skepticism causes a violent break between her and her old partner. Yet in her most dazzling flights concerning the life and times of Mrs. Harris, Mrs. Gamp's craving for money and drink can, without the slightest effect on her fancy, intrude the most realistic demands: " 'Mrs. Gamp,' she says in answer, 'if ever there was a sober creetur to be got at eighteenpence a day for working people, and three-and-six for gentlefolks — night-watching,' " said Mrs. Gamp, with emphasis, " 'being a extra charge — you are that inwallable person.' " Mrs. Gamp's eye being on the main chance, she quotes Mrs. Harris only to impress other people, for the sake of gain or kudos; unlike some other comic characters whose invention stops far short of a Mrs. Harris, she does not carry her dramatic imagining into soliloquies. Dickens' talkers, for that matter, are seldom alone.

Mrs. Nickleby, Mr. Swiveller, and Mrs. Gamp can hardly be said to represent an "idea" in the mind of their creator (unless Mrs. Gamp embodies a sort of early demand for Florence Nightingales), but Mr. and Mrs. Micawber do represent an idea. In addition to being themselves (and to being more or less Mr. and Mrs. John Dickens), they are a dramatic objectification of Dickens' fervent hatred of Malthusianism and Utilitarianism. The pair are unpractical, improvident, polyphiloprogenitive, in every way unfitted for survival in a world of competition; but they are also, in their own peculiar way, above that world. Moreover, in his occasional sober moments, Mr. Micawber has a philosophy, which of course he does not practise; his summary of the relations of income and expenditure to happiness and misery has long been classic. What is more important, at one sober moment he displays — without sentimentality — a depth of feeling and a dignity that we remember through all his troubles and absurdities. Just before one statement of that economic principle, when his censure of procrastination has evoked from his wife a reference to poor papa's maxim, Mr. Micawber pronounces a loyal if limited eulogy over his late father-in-law and continues:

> "But he applied that maxim to our marriage, my dear; and that was so far prematurely entered into, in consequence, that I never recovered the expense."
>
> Mr. Micawber looked aside at Mrs. Micawber, and added, "Not that I am sorry for it. Quite the contrary, my love." After which he was grave for a minute or two.

A few paragraphs later, Mrs. Micawber, looking down at David from the top of the coach, sees how small the sharer of their trials is, and beckons him to climb up for a warm and motherly kiss. Because of such moments the Micawbers are not mere figures of fun.

The mental assets of the Micawbers — they have no others — are partly divided. Though both have the resiliency they so greatly need, Mr. Micawber possesses the exuberant dramatic imagination; his wife, it appears, the cool, logical intellect. Mrs. Micawber is much worse off than Mrs. Nickleby, and more acutely aware of her situation, and her frequent glances back to her life with papa are not a happy escape from the present but a painful contrast. Mrs. Micawber's logical faculty has not altogether extinguished her instinct for self-dramatization; this comes out both in her sincerely theatrical protestations of attachment to her husband and in her tendency to make a public occasion of her own and her family's history: "My papa lived to bail Mr. Micawber several times, and then expired, regretted by a numerous circle." Mr. Micawber is able to live much more buoyantly in the moment and in the future, and his instinct for turning private into public drama is much more richly developed. This instinct is perhaps the armor that keeps him almost invulnerable and almost always happy. If he has nothing else to sustain him, there is his own eloquence. On his lips a chain of rotund clichés lights up the world. His habit of adding a plain statement, by way of translation, to his rolling periods is a sort of concession to the requirements of everyday intercourse (though even these brevities are dramatically rendered), yet his own essential life is lived, as it were, on the platform and the stage. Any audience will do, from little David to his fellow inmates of the debtors' prison or the people assembled for the unmasking of Heep. Whether listening to his own voice, or making flourishes at his throat with a razor, or drinking punch, or leading his family along the Medway with the coal trade in view, Mr. Micawber lives in his imagination, and the slings and arrows of outrageous fortune cannot wound him.

Mr. and Mrs. Micawber seem to be thought of as the last of Dickens' great comic characters, those characters who, by virtue of their dimensions and vitality, have an existence independent of the books in a sort of Platonic heaven. In the later novels, whether because of some lessening of the author's fecundity or because of his seeking a more disciplined organic structure, his comic (and other) characters are nearer life size and their prodigal self-revelations are held in check. Comedy goes on, but the procession no longer includes people who stand out as far larger than life. For instance, Herbert Pocket, Pip's friend, is just such a hopeful and unsuccessful young man "in the City" as the young Micawber would have been; but Herbert is a subdued and relatively normal person. On the other hand, if Mrs. Gamp's Mrs. Harris represents the Cockney dream world, what shall we say of that split personality, Mr. Wemmick, who makes such a realistic-fantastic division between his half-mechanized life in the Newgate world of Mr. Jaggers' office and his human life at Walworth in the minute castle with the drawbridge, the cannon, and the Aged?

We have been recalling a few of the most famous figures in Dickens, mainly the earlier Dickens, but a host of people in all the books — sometimes even nameless people — have in some degree the instinct for dramatizing themselves. At the very beginning of *Pickwick Papers*, Mr. Pickwick's cabman, suspecting the motive behind his passenger's innocent questions about his horse, puts on an act in giving extravagant answers — though at the end of the journey his workaday self is manifested in his appeal to fists. In *Edwin Drood* the drunken Durdles registers, or enlarges, his place in the scheme of things by referring to himself, very favorably, in the third person. A full list of examples between these two chronological poles would run almost into a Dickens dictionary. Perhaps the chief groups of exceptions would be the wholly respectable and ultra-good characters, who are, often unhappily, their simple selves. The self-dramatizing instinct is especially strong in the multitude of the lower middle and lower class. Their usually drab and commonplace lives do not give scope for their vitality and imagination and they consciously or unconsciously create for themselves a more exciting or glamorous role. Many of them are, by conventional standards, failures, and not at all sublime failures, but ridiculous and pathetic — like Mr. Wopsle, "the celebrated Provincial Amateur of Roscian renown." Such a vision might have invited sentimentality, yet, however ready Dickens was to respond in other areas, he seldom did in this; there is enough realistic detail to disinfect, enough humor to irradiate, such figures. They belong partly to Victorian England, partly to fairyland. George Orwell, who saw truly so much of Dickens, but whose moral boiling point was rather low, startles us when he pronounces Micawber "a cadging scoundrel"; surely one might as well call Jack the Giant-Killer a homicidal maniac.

It is agreed that Dickens could not deal satisfactorily with love on its common levels, much less with grand passions; yet he could deal, incomparably, with love of the off-beat kind (witness the chapter on the married life of David and his feckless child-wife, which Gissing thought a perfect piece of writing). Dickens could discern a chivalric knight-errant in the soul of an eccentric, frustrated nobody, a divine spark in the wooden Barkis, in the almost equally inarticulate adorer of Florence Dombey, Mr. Toots, in the Walworth side of Mr. Wemmick. Most of these absurd and genuine lovers cast themselves, with varying degrees of consciousness, in romantic roles (even Barkis has his moments of almost wordless drama). The clerks at Mrs. Todgers' boardinghouse, roused to new levels of emotion by the disturbing presence of the Pecksniff girls, carry on high feuds with theatrical grandiosity. Mr. Guppy, though his devotion to Esther Summerson does not extinguish his legal prudence ("Half a minute, miss! . . . This has been without prejudice?"), haunts the theatre when she goes there, in a state of woeful dejection, his hair flattened with bear's grease. And along with such lovers must be put the good-hearted Flora Finching, whose coy stream-of-consciousness speeches fail of their effect on Arthur Clennam.

Disappointed lovers are only one category. Countless miscellaneous people have a positive enjoyment in being their dramatic selves (like Betsey Trotwood), or in heightening themselves, playing a bigger role than life has granted them. And the instinct is not limited to the comic. It gives a half-comic note to many villains or near-villains; it animates Squeers and Mantalini, the demonic Quilp and the pious Pecksniff, the windy Chadband and the courtly Turveydrop. Old Krook's playing the part of a Lord Chancellor becomes symbolic satire; Harold Skimpole's role of childlike dilettante ends in base duplicity. (There is no comedy at all in John Jasper's gravitating between the cathedral organ-loft and the opium den.) Indeed the dramatic instinct, which in the Swivellers and Micawbers is pure *joie de vivre*, a sort of comic existentialism, may, in their social superiors, be pure knavery. In all the books, and increasingly in the later ones, most people of the higher levels are acting a part and engaged in some kind of conscious deception.

But that is another story. So too is Dickens' constant endowment of inanimate objects with dramatic life. This has long been recognized as a hallmark of the Dickensian manner in ordinary and incidental description, and of late years it has been more and more recognized as a conscious symbolic device. To mention one of the innumerable examples, the casts of the swollen faces of two hanged convicts in Mr. Jaggers' office seem to Pip, every time he calls, to be alive and attentive, and they become in his mind brutal symbols of evil and the law.

This paper, however, has been only a glance at human comedy, and at one quality in that, a quality so self-evident that there is small excuse for talking about it, except for the pleasure of doing so.

Sex in the Modern Novel

I AM GETTING TIRED of reading current novels, and I do not think I am alone in that. It may be only the familiar experience of surviving into an alien — and conceivably a wiser — generation, of growing old and crabbed. That is perhaps not the only reason, yet the odds are heavily against anyone who would suggest others. To discuss the technical methods of current highbrow fiction and to deal in the impressive clichés of the age of violence is to be an intellectual in good standing. But to ask if current fiction, highbrow and lowbrow alike, does not provide a surfeit of sex and sensationalism is to expose oneself as an antique of softened brain and hardened arteries. Before such a prospect strong men blench.

However, as Juvenal said, the penniless traveler whistles in the face of the highwayman, and one who has no claims to being an intellectual cannot be read out of the party. A case could probably be made for some dimness of moral vision in both conventional novelists and their conventionally approving critics, but a more strategic ground for complaint might be found in artistic considerations alone. One may then set forth the proposition that our novelists' common and exclusive concern with sex grows out of an unrealistically and inartistically narrow conception of the novel (if not of life) and that the common fictional prod-

Reprinted from *The Atlantic Monthly*, January 1959.

ucts are inexpressibly monotonous and tedious. These and subsequent remarks have to do not with exceptions but with general tendencies both in subcritical fiction and in the serious writing that may be thought to suffer from the prevalent contagion as well as from a partly misguided literary creed. Further, these remarks are not prompted by the recent sensation, *Lolita*, which is too well written and astringent to deserve the cruder labels thrown at it but which can hardly disown the label of abnormal psychology.

Although the freedom of utterance that came with or brought about the decay of censorship was hailed as the arrival of American adulthood, a frequent result has been a regression to adolescence; or perhaps the exploitation of unadulterated sex should be called a new toy. It used to be that the curious reader in quest of the risqué had to go to the scrofulous French novel, but how pallid it was and is, compared with the modern native product. If, a century from now, the social historian should read many best sellers of our time, he would be forced to conclude that male and female Americans of this period were wholly engaged in amorous and extramarital affairs, with incidental excursions into business, politics, war, and so forth. For nowadays affairs are as automatic in a novel as corpses in a detective story; the only question is how many are required. The emotional and moral tension that might be set up by an effort at self-control hardly comes into the contemporary view of human nature.

In that charming old idyl, *The Vicar of Wakefield*, the innocent vicar early announces that "all our adventures were by the fireside, and all our migrations from the blue bed to the brown." This last phrase, somewhat reinterpreted, may serve to summarize a mass of modern and especially American fiction. Everyman and Everywoman seek their souls' salvation through a pilgrimage from bed to bed, and the more laps the race entails the finer is the resultant spiritual integrity. But there is a degree of sameness. After one has absorbed a dozen modish novels, one becomes an expert in the routine and the patter. This is, to be sure, subject to variations — you may have clinically anatomical reporting with a pseudomystical shimmer, or clinically anatomical reporting without a shimmer — but in general it runs in a standard groove. The resources of the human anatomy and vocabulary being alike limited, no one can really win the Frankness Stakes, and the contest, however profitable for author and publisher, is for the adult spectator a considerable bore.

The decorum of a family magazine hardly permits a parody, but, since the same close observation of life and the same fearless honesty are carried into the rare glimpses we are given of nonsexual activities, one might compose a sample, in such an innocuous area, of one popular technique:

> I reached for my shoe and pulled it on with a jerk. It split over the base of the big toe. I began to lace it. The lace broke. I stood up and poured myself a drink. It burned my throat. I hunted for another lace. There wasn't one in the drawer. I tied the broken pieces together. The knot wouldn't go through the eyelet. I took another stiff drink. The sky turned purple. A bird sang outside.

In case the gentle reader misses the complex point, it may be explained that this grim vignette symbolizes the crushing weight of the modern industrial megalopolis, the shoddiness of its standardized manufactures and civilization, and the lonely desperation of the frustrated individual unable to realize himself in a stagnant and repressive society, a desperation barely mitigated by possibilities of Dionysiac rebirth. But this technique, as I said, must be shifted to the realm of sex. In the current novel all human drives and needs and activities must be channeled into sexual terms, must be translated, as it were, into the Basic of our time, and into many, many pages.

"Oh," says the modernist, "you want our writers to be like the nineteenth-century novelists, from Jane Austen to James, who never used a word that, as Dickens' Mr. Podsnap said, would bring a blush to the cheek of the young person." Of course no one would want to revert to the rigorous propriety that Mrs. Grundy demanded from those novelists (and that irked some of them), and we may rejoice in the new freedom, even if it has not yet given birth to many novelists comparable in stature to the older ones. But to say this is not to grant that our self-conscious, stereotyped, blow-by-blow recording of incessant sexual encounters is artistically more effective than the method of reticent suggestion. Would Becky Sharp be in the slightest degree more vivid in her corruption, or would Sir Pitt Crawley and Lord Steyne have any more satyrlike actuality, if they had been handled in the modern manner? Mature readers are interested in feelings, states of mind.

But if the modernist, who is no less rigorous in his way than Mrs. Grundy was in hers, insists that most of the older British and American novelists were squeamish and mealy-mouthed, we might think of the other great novelists of the century who cannot be charged with minimizing sex — Stendhal, Balzac, and Flaubert, Dostoevsky, Turgenev, and Tolstoy. So far as I remember, not one of these went in for seeing and telling all. Notwithstanding the portentous examples of Joyce and D. H. Lawrence, one may argue that, whether a novelist is depicting joyful ecstasy or joyless lust or a complex mixture of emotions, the piling up of physical detail constitutes, as a rule, a failure rather than a triumph of imaginative understanding and communication. To go a long way back, Virgil's brief account of the meeting of Venus and Vulcan has been justly described as one of the most sensual passages in all literature:

> ille repente
> accepit solitam flammam, notusque medullas
> intravit calor et labefacta per ossa cucurrit;

yet the means employed are no less reticent than potent.

But if the method of suggestion, though it has been the method of almost all the great masters, be questioned by modern practitioners and critics, there can hardly be any question about the overwhelming and myopic concentration on the theme of sex in modern novels. And, for our present concern, themes and attitudes are more important than methods. Sex, being a universal and urgent force in human nature and life, is inevitably and rightly a central theme of literature. Moreover, even the most squalid levels belong to the writer's proper world, though one could ask if emphasis on those levels represents a rational and aesthetic balance; but that question may be passed by. Instead, taking sex in all its manifestations, we might ask if current concentration on that theme provides anything like a rounded picture of life. Such a narrowly limited vision is not found in any of the great novelists from Cervantes to those of the twentieth century.

Is the ignoring or slighting of sex in the older British and American novels a greater distortion of life than the ignoring or slighting of everything except sex? The French and Russian novelists, who enjoyed more freedom than those of Britain and the United States, treated sex as one element in the immensely varied patterns and confusions of the human psyche and society. To run over their names, and the

British and American names as well, is to be reminded of the infinite wealth of themes and material and characters they embraced and created: national strife, all kinds of moral problems, the comedy of manners and morals, the pursuit of money or power, social oppression and revolt. One can hardly count up the areas and levels of individual and social experience that make up the totality of life, areas and levels which the older novelists got into their books and which seem to be deliberately excluded from the world of most of the newer modern writers. Many of the older novelists even dealt with love — and not merely love between man and woman but all the relationships that go under that name.

One readily imagines of course all sorts of indignant replies. Perhaps the most obvious would be, "Life is like that." Well, some parts of life have always been like that, but, if we must rely on individual testimony, the many great older novelists, as we have observed, did not see any such one-sided picture. One significant contrast, by the way, between the older fiction and ours is that, while our writers would go to the stake rather than sentimentalize (or perhaps even admit) a good character, they have not the slightest hesitation about sentimentalizing the bad — if one may use such simple categories as signposts.

There are many other possible replies. "We know that only a part of life is like that, but Freud and Company have focused the modern mind on sex as the matrix and medium of all human interests, and the activities that other novelists treated per se we are bound to render in sexual terms." "The American bourgeois scene is in the main so respectably dull that it cannot generate a passion, an emotional crisis, and art must deal with characters who can be passionate." "In a world newly accustomed to wholesale brutality we have to use shock tactics; people nowadays have no ear for the still small voice of Jane Austen or James." "In the modern world the individual is consciously or unconsciously the victim of forces that he is powerless to alter; the novelist, confronted with the enormous complexities of life, can study only private behavior." "The old capacious novel of manners is extinct; one must conform to the current vogue." "There is no use in talking about what an artist should or should not do; he can only put down what he sees and feels; if you can't see the truth he tells, it is not his fault." "Of course the novelist cherishes moral values as much as anybody, though he is groping toward new and more valid ones; anyhow, the sophisticated writer has to present these by indirection and implication." And so on.

The serious modern novel doubtless commands an enthusiastic following, considerable in intelligence if not in numbers (not to mention the millions who follow pornographic lures). But it may be thought that such defenses as have been suggested do not add up to a convincing argument. This is not the first and only age in which mankind has lived with a half-paralyzing consciousness of disorder, though a number of intellectuals seem to have a defective historical sense and to assume that life on this earth was fairly rosy until a generation ago. Moreover, our world being in a very bad way because people feel and act as they do, one might raise the naive question of why our extreme candor about sex is attended by such extreme reticence about virtue; novelists may be reluctant to hazard guesses as to what that is and how it works. The emphasis on sex and sensation may be related not only to moral dubiety but to lack of creative power; a reader cannot respond sympathetically to people embroiled in messes if they do not come alive as persons but remain figures moved about in accordance with an abstract diagram. If it is urged that American life is so oppressively standardized that sex is the only area in which individuality can assert itself, it may be answered that such self-assertion has become as standardized as anything else, that rebellion against convention is the most effete of conventions; and, if sex is made the vehicle for the whole complex of human experience, it is quite inadequate and much too easy.

Perhaps the best answer to all pros and cons would be the appearance of a new novelist big enough to create characters of vitality and dignity and to grasp many strands of life, as the older novelists commonly did and as Boris Pasternak has lately done; one might even entertain the bizarre notion of a novelist's touching on the beauty of goodness. Assuredly novelists are free to, are obliged to, obey their compulsive vision (though one is not sure that this vision, even for writers of integrity, is unaffected by fashion). But readers are free too, and a number of them have had more than enough of changes rung on aggressive, sensual, frenetic egoism, whether it is or is not enveloped in a haze of sentimental morality. The critics who predict the doom of the novel, for subtler reasons than are offered here, may be right; one hopes not. Meanwhile some intelligent people are turning to the older novelists, to biography, history, science, perhaps even to poetry; they want something that the current novel seldom gives. It is conceivable that they have reason.

Hands Across the Sea

SOME YEARS AGO I received an interesting letter from an Oxford undergraduate. He had, he said, just sent me a bale of copies of a magazine he and his friends had started: would I distribute quotas of these to bookshops in Cambridge (Massachusetts) and, after a reasonable time, collect unsold copies and return them to him? As compensation for my trouble I might keep five percent of the proceeds. My feelings probably do not need to be described: there is a limit to elderly charity, if not to young ambition. I confess, however, that, while metaphorically biting nails, I forced myself to think of the dreams of youth, and I did meekly and weakly trot around to bookshops with this miserable magazine; and I did collect and return unsold copies, with the money for, I think, two. Such a commission is, one may imagine and hope, unique in Anglo-American annals. As I plodded on my rounds, I wondered among other things what would have happened in the way of cosmic explosions if a student in the United States had shown such brash effrontery toward an Oxford professor; but one could hardly conceive of that.

The fact is that in England the colonial attitude has not yet altogether died out. Most academic Britons, men and women — to stick to the limited world I know — are, intellectually and personally, the salt of the earth, at home or

Reprinted from *The American Scholar*, Summer 1964.

abroad. When they visit the United States they respond with eager interest to ways that are different from their own; they do not patronize and do not throw their weight about. They are well aware of the large American contribution to the world's intellectual stores and draw upon it when they write themselves. With such people, good citizens of the international commonwealth of intellect and letters, this little piece has nothing to do — except by way of warm salutation. But there is a small minority who do much to turn the academic American's normal Anglophilia into Anglophobia, whether they set off verbal firecrackers at home or appear in person to civilize the natives. These are in all respects the reverse of the good friends briefly described above; they dislike all things American, miss the rightness of all things English, and accept everything that is done for them as only their due, or perhaps less. While some visiting Britons give admirable lectures, these others evidently think that anything will do for the backwoods and offer what an American would not present to a freshman class. One noteworthy lecture I did not hear but heard of: an eminent scientist read, from a journal he held in his hand, an article he had published a couple of years earlier. We may wonder if he would have welcomed as payment a canceled check. It is almost a century since James Russell Lowell wrote of a certain condescension in foreigners, and in his time there was much stronger ground for it — if the ground for condescension is ever strong — than there is now; but, as I say, some English people are still living in that or an earlier period.

Complacent insularity manifests itself in a variety of ways, small and large. A short time ago I had a letter from an English university official addressed to me at "Harvard University, Harvard, Illinois" — as one might say "Oxford

University, Boston, Lincolnshire." So far as I am aware, Americans do not propose themselves for posts at Oxford and Cambridge and London, but some English dons of less than exalted standing have no qualms about offering their services to major American universities. One case, although it goes back a good many years, is too remarkable to pass by: a certain worthy scholar, being old and in need and fuzzy in mind, was shipped off by zealous friends to be head of a department in a Canadian university, where presumably the state of his intellect would not be noticed. (A couple of items might be added: the aged professor, knowing only that he was bound for Kingston, was increasingly perturbed when told, on several successive days, that his ship was moving up the Gulf of St. Lawrence, so that he finally burst out, "But there can't be a river of this size in Jamaica!"; later, having gone to another city to lecture, he failed to appear on the platform, and a hasty search party found him in his quarters, lying in the bathtub and placidly reading *The Vicar of Wakefield.*) One small but revealing bit of insularity is a quaint locution often met in the reviewing and advertising columns of English periodicals: an American book is said to be by "the professor" of history or English or whatnot in his university. Because English universities have traditionally had one "professor" at the top of the departmental hierarchy, it is assumed that all other universities must have followed that pattern, although the American author may be one of a score of professors in his department. One remembers that good old tale of the English newspaper headline, "Storm in the Channel: Continent Isolated." Complacent insularity can be highly imaginative. For another random but specific item one might quote a fantastic statement from an article on the reprint of *Scrutiny*, about "H. A. Mason's book on Humanism and Poetry, which began a new phase in comparative literature, and which is in no small measure responsible for the current revival of classical studies in the U.S.A." (*The Listener*, January 9, 1964, p. 63).

Some English people who have taught or resided for a term or two at one of the lesser American universities can — even if they don't write college novels still stranger than our own — cherish and propagate mirthful memories of students who in knowledge and literacy were far below those of Oxbridge. Professor Marcus Cunliffe, in a relatively knowledgeable account of Harvard and American universities in general (*Encounter*, January 1960), spoke of mediocrity as if it were peculiar to the United States and quite unknown in England. The fact of frequent inferiority may be granted, since American universities take in a vastly greater proportion of the young, but the conventional comparison is not very logical. The lower ranks of American students should be compared, not with those of Oxbridge (of redbrick standards I know nothing), but with the mass of English youth who receive no formal education at all beyond school (granted also the frequent although by no means uniform superiority of English schools). If Oxbridge is to be the standard, the logical comparison would be with good students at the major American universities and colleges, and these, I think, would not suffer. (I might remark that in courses of my own I have had English graduates both of Oxford and Cambridge who called Donne "Don.") Americans may not have the same degree of specialized knowledge, since they must spend part of their time on areas outside their own; but in England of late there seems to be increased questioning of narrowly professional specialization and some feeling that the broader American theory and practice may be sound.

It would seem, on the face of it, a very dubious assumption that an English student, at school or the university or through private enterprise, gets a real equivalent of the American student's acquaintance with literature, history, philosophy, the natural and social sciences, and the fine arts.

To judge from the evidence in print, although there is perhaps less than there used to be, gibes at the American Ph.D. are still current coin in English common rooms and at cocktail parties. Since few English people have any actual knowledge of the program or have ever read a thesis, the topic has the advantage Sir Robert Walpole found in bawdy talk at the table, that all can join in on equal terms. An eminent English scholar once said to me, with the tart finality of a schoolmaster adressing a young culprit: "You don't fail nearly enough candidates." Whatever degree of truth or error this assertion contained, the speaker had no way of knowing anything about our examinations; British superiority was simply an unquestionable fact of life. Some years ago an Oxford professor wrote to the *Times Literary Supplement* to report with amazement and horror that American oral examinations concerned themselves with the basic experience of literature; apparently we should stick to really serious things like bibliography.

The *Times Literary Supplement*, while notably cordial toward American creative writing, has often been less than cordial toward American literary scholarship. For a recent attack (June 28, 1963) it brought up its heavy artillery, a middle article of nearly four columns and an editorial of nearly two — all this by way of demolishing an American thesis on social criticism found in doggerel verse of the later nineteenth century. While the reviewer admitted that this book was "a pretty extreme case," both he and the writer of the editorial — and various later correspondents — took it as a sufficient basis for large and lordly generalizations about the American academic elders "under whose rule these atrocities are committed." As is usual in polemics of this kind, the extreme case rapidly became the normal. This sort of thing, said the editorial, is "bedevilling a wide range of human thought, particularly, it seems, in the United States." Twenty or thirty years ago, we were told, a few theses were written in England, most of them pieces of original research; they were seldom printed, and, when they were, they were more or less indistinguishable from an ordinary book. Well, if one were so minded, one could write a similar article about academic diseases in England, building likewise on one extreme case, a case dating in fact from those good old days of original research: I remember a published English thesis that tabulated the novels of Hardy in order according to the amount of "gloom" and other elements they contained.

If the champions of better things had been concerned about the truth, they could have learned from the annual bibliographies of recent years that most American doctoral theses are philosophic and aesthetic interpretations of literature that matters; but facts would have checked the free flow of censorious fancy. Of the very large quantity of American scholarly and critical publication — some of it certainly done by immature persons under forced draft — there is of course a portion that should not have been published, or perhaps written, but that is not peculiar to the United States; it looms larger here than elsewhere because a great many more people are engaged in scholarly activities. And, however regrettable such wasted effort is from every point of view, it does not vitiate the high proportion of more or less valuable writing. We may note, too, that, if relatively few doctoral theses are published in England, there have long been books of another and not much better kind that is relatively rare in the United States — that is, superficial popularizations, especially biographies, which contain little or nothing fresh and exist mainly as nice entertainment, and which — as I have remarked elsewhere — are written not only for but by the general reader.

There is in this contrast the element of "Gentlemen vs. Professionals." The amateur tradition in England has a long, honorable, and attractive history, but the modern scholar or critic is bound to be professional if he is to be at all adequate; and during this past generation professionalism has grown rapidly in England, with mainly happy results. The best English scholars and critics are well informed on American and other foreign work. But the insularity of amateurism still appears in books that purport to address people above the general reader. Again and again one still finds the assumption that nothing of importance can have been written outside of England. The consequence is that some English books of scholarly pretensions are out-of-date before they are published.

Anti-American feeling — which owes more or less to resentment over the American position in world affairs — has one cathartic outlet in the reviewing of American books, especially books of literary scholarship and criticism. Some good American as well as English books are praised, and some poor English as well as American books are damned, but there has long been a discernible tendency to damn more or less good American books on general principles. One gets the impression that, for some English reviewers, the prime question is not "Is this a good or a bad book?" but "Is this book by an Englishman or an American?" There is a stock of derogatory adjectives for automatic use on American books — dull, laborious, uninspired, pedantic, ill-written, and so on. And quite often the reviewer who derides the book reveals, along with ingrained prejudice, a shallow acquaintance with the subject. I once sent a note of protest about a review of a notably able work (not by me) that has since taken its place among standard books. The reviewer had devoted one half of his space to denouncing the book and the other half to denouncing American scholarship in general. When I wrote later to ask why my note had not been printed, the editor replied that he could not take account of every little chauvinistic outburst. One would have thought that the guilt of chauvinism lay elsewhere.

Of course we Americans love England, many English people, and English literature, which is our heritage also. But now and then we think that the sour few might look inward instead of across the sea, might ask themselves if a complacent sense of superiority is well founded, if they have scrapped the once celebrated spirit of "British fair play," and if they can afford to throw so many pebbles or brickbats when they live in a country where, for instance, Mr. Robert Graves (however fine a poet) delivers at Cambridge and Oxford lectures that embarrass even the solitary reader, where highbrow critics greeted Mr. Colin Wilson as a major prophet, where Lord Snow, as universal sage, dispenses amiable judgments on anything, where devout disciples of Dr. Leavis regard him with a reverence almost equal to his own, and where Dr. Rowse plays such fantastic tricks before high heaven as make the angels laugh.

Calculus Racked Him

TO JUDGE FROM A GOOD many recent publications, small and large, in the serious study of Renaissance poetry the wave of the future is to be occult numerology (or, more properly, arithmology). The prospect disposes me to welcome retirement — a feeling that doubtless places me as a blind reactionary. No one of course would dispute the fact of the long tradition of Pythagorean-Platonic-Christian symbolism, a theory — like the Ptolemaic cosmos — much embellished and complicated over the centuries. But it is quite another matter to impose the theory arbitrarily upon particular poets and poems when there is no evidence that a given poet had any such esoteric interest or knowledge, much less an inclination to build poems on symbolic numbers — or that, if he had, he could have expected many understanding readers. I should like to look at one example of the new learning, "The Hidden Sense: Milton and the Neoplatonic Method of Numerical Composition."[1] The author, Miss Røstvig, has substantial and rational books to her credit, but even a seasoned and sober scholar can evidently be intoxicated by the spongy air of dazzling spells and blear illusion.

Reprinted by permission from *Studies in English Literature* (Rice University), Winter 1966.

[1] Maren-Sofie Røstvig et al., *The Hidden Sense and Other Essays*, Norwegian Studies in English, No. 9 (New York, 1963).

Miss Røstvig quotes medieval and Renaissance authorities on the science of numbers, and, apart from her main subject, Milton, she gives more or less space to Du Bartas, Donne, Chapman, Spenser, and Henry More; an epilogue brings in James Joyce. We might linger a minute with Donne, since he is one familiar figure who shows his knowledge of the tradition, and since Miss Røstvig's brief discussion of him is judicious. Near the beginning of his *Essays in Divinity* Donne refers to two principal interpreters of numbers, Pico della Mirandola and Francesco Giorgio, and joins "most" people in dismissing such "Cabalistick learning" as vanity. However, as Miss Røstvig says, he does indulge in a section "Of Number," and touches especially the historical significance of 70; but he ends with a Christian warning against such overcurious speculations. Miss Røstvig makes no claim for Donne's poetic use of numbers except in *The Primrose*, "which exploits the symbolic implications of 4, 5, 6, and 10." Miss Røstvig further observes that in this poem each stanza has 10 lines divided into 4 lines of 6 syllables and 6 of 10 syllables. But she is much more cautious here in regard to numerical structure than she is in dealing with Milton; her account of him is, like the profusion of Eden, "Wild above rule or art."

Miss Røstvig cites Milton's early prolusion on the music of the spheres, but that universal commonplace is not evidence for any concern with symbolic numbers. Otherwise, Miss Røstvig (pp. 41f) finds his "only direct reference to the science of numbers . . . in his discussion of the Sabbath" (*Christian Doctrine*, II.vii: Columbia edition, XVII, 183). Here, apropos of the seventh day, Milton denies that a particular number possesses any inherent virtue or efficacy. This assertion, which Miss Røstvig records with commendable candor, would seem to be a troublesome obstacle in the way of her approach to Milton. She gets around it by appealing to his account of creation, where he says that matter is "a passive principle, dependent on the Deity, and subservient to him *as in the case of numbers*" (XV, 18). Here Miss Røstvig avowedly differs from the Columbia translator, who is, I think, more correct in following the total logic of the sentence: "seeing that it [matter] is only a passive principle, dependent on the Deity, and subservient to him; and seeing, moreover, that, as in number, considered abstractedly, so also in time or eternity there is no inherent force or efficacy. . . ." In any case, Miss Røstvig's version of this clause hardly converts Milton's explicit rejection of symbolic numbers into acceptance.

From this premise we are to proceed with confidence. For general conceptions and particular symbolic numbers Miss Røstvig cites Cassiodorus' *Institutiones*, Francesco Giorgio's *De harmonia mundi*, Cornelius Agrippa's *De occulta philosophia*, and other works; the three named, especially the last two, are seen as probable sources for Milton. In this twilight area reason is freed from normal restrictions. Thus Milton's division of the *Christian Doctrine* into two books "is tantamount to a rejection of that Trinity which the book itself rejects in no uncertain terms" (p. 39). We may wonder if Sir Thomas Browne, the Christian Platonist so notably inclined to mystical symbolism, was likewise rejecting the Trinity when he divided *Religio Medici* into two books also given to divinity and ethics. Like Cassiodorus, Milton divided his first book into 33 chapters (the number of years of Christ's life); the 17 chapters of the second book probably "represent Augustine's analysis of the number 17 as the sum of the ten commandments and the seven gifts of the Holy Ghost" (p. 40).

Milton's *Art of Logic* similarly has two books of 33 and 17 chapters respectively: here the numbers "underline the connection between the art of reasoning and God, working through the Word and the Holy Ghost."

To come to the poems, Miss Røstvig deals chiefly with the *Nativity* and *Comus*, and we may look chiefly at the first. She builds (pp. 43f) on "the Platonic exposition of creation in numerical terms, according to which all numbers proceed from the One until we reach the cube of the first and the first even number. This may be diagrammed as follows:

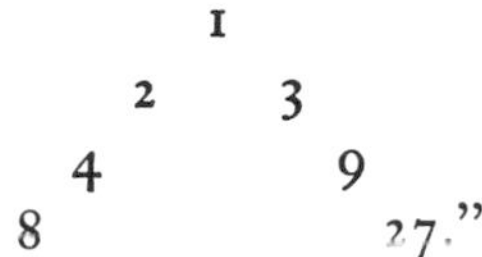

Miss Røstvig believes "that the structure of Milton's Nativity Ode is patterned after this Platonic *lambda*, its 27 8-line stanzas representing the two impulses issuing from the One" (p. 44).

"The Nativity Ode consists of an introduction and a hymn, the former totalling 4 7-line stanzas and 28 lines, the latter 27 8-line stanzas and 216 lines" (p. 54). The numbers of the introduction (4, 7, 28) point to the world of time, the sequence of weeks, months, and seasons (4 elements, humors, passions, seasons, etc.; 7, the number of the moon's planetary sphere, of the ages of man, etc.; 28 days in a month, the sum of the numbers from 1 to 7, etc.). The number 4 is pre-eminently the number of the created universe, so the 4-stanza introduction suitably symbolized Christ's becoming flesh. Since the age yielded presumably some hundreds of poems in 4 stanzas, the possibilities become overwhelming; we might think, for instance, of the different kind of fleshliness in Donne's *Communitie*, *The Curse*, *The Broken Heart*; or of the same numbers, 4, 7, and 28, in Donne's *The Undertaking*, *A Feaver*, *The Baite* (7 4-line stanzas), and *Loves Deitie* (4 7-line stanzas). Since 4 is the number of the created universe, we might note that Donne's *Elegie XVIII* (*Loves Progress*) has 4 paragraphs containing respectively 16, 20, 36, and 24 lines, all multiples of 4. Carew's *A Rapture* is a less perfect example; it has 6 paragraphs, of 20, 34, 24, 36, 32, and 20 lines, all except the second being multiples of 4. The second paragraph, however, is not a fatal impediment, since 34 = 2 × 17, and we know already that 17 can represent the sum of the ten commandments and the seven gifts of the Holy Ghost.

Still dealing with the introduction, Miss Røstvig observes (p. 55): "If we count the number of feet and syllables in each stanza, we arrive at 36 — the great tetractys — and 72, which denotes the complete cycle of years attributed to the life of man from birth to death." The metronome of mystical metrics apparently disregards slurred and hypermetric syllables (as in lines 7, 8, and 10) which would alter the total of 72.

The same mixture of loose and Procrustean argument appears in Miss Røstvig's discussion of the Hymn. The change to 8-line stanzas "means that we leave the world of time (the cosmic week of seven ages within which the history of fallen man is acted out) for the eighth age of the reign of Christ. The hymn is completely dominated by numbers expressive of perfection, timelessness, and harmony, 8 and 27 being the most important ones" (p. 56). The fact is that, apart from brief reference to eternity, the whole Hymn is occupied with the world of time, from the Creation to the Judgment; the theme of the first third is the imperfection of nature, and that theme persists, in contrast with heavenly perfection, throughout. But let us look at the numbers, 27 stanzas of 8 lines each, making a total of 216 lines: ". . . 8 symbolises the passive matter out of which the hymn is created by means of the active principle of form symbolised by the cube of 3" (p. 57). To be more concrete, "The number of heavy stresses in each stanza is 32, the number of syllables 64 — numbers which represent justice according to Pythagoras. . . ." (p. 58). Marvell's *The Garden* is thus apparently involved with justice too, since it has 32 stresses and 64 syllables in each stanza and, besides, has 72 lines (72 denoting, as we saw, the life cycle of man). But "heavy stresses" make a dubious foundation for precise statistics, since different readers may get different results; Miss Røstvig seems to take a uniform number for granted. According to my count of the first ten stanzas of Milton's Hymn, only six have 32 stresses, only three have 64 syllables, and only one (stanza iv) has 32 plus 64, which Miss Røstvig gives as the fixed combination for all 27 stanzas. While another person's count might differ slightly from mine, it would appear that "justice," as usual, limps on halting feet.

The unreliable statistics somewhat weaken the concluding summary (even if the pyramid of cubes had any significance): "Finally it may be mentioned that the product of the two cubes, 8 and 27, is 216 — which in its turn is the cube of 6. The total number of lines therefore forms a number signifying perfection kept steady in three-dimensional security. We have, then, cubed figures everywhere — the cube of 2 in the number of lines per stanza, the cube of 3 in the number of stanzas, the cube of 4 in the number of syllables in each stanza, and the cube of 6 in the total number of lines; everywhere perfection is in this manner made permanent and lasting" (p. 58). There are also 216 lines in that poem of insecurity, Jonson's *Execration upon Vulcan.*

The second main subject is *Comus*. Before we come to the business of numbers we might notice Miss Røstvig's argument (p. 61) that in lines 359–85 and 418–75, on the chastity and corruption of the soul, Milton is close to Agrippa. He may have read Agrippa, but every student knows that in part of the second passage Milton is paraphrasing *Phaedo* 80–81, which Miss Røstvig does not mention. Another parallel is that "Milton refers to 'backward mutters of dissevering power' (line 817) as a means of freeing the Lady, while Agrippa notes that orations pronounced backwards produce unusual effects" (p. 62). Again it is a commonplace of editorial annotation that Milton is following the story of Circe in Ovid, *Metamorphoses*, xiv.300–1. Many of her parallels, says Miss Røstvig, "are too general to suggest indebtedness, but the accumulative effect is nevertheless impressive"; that is, many nothings add up to something. But in regard to the magic power of numbers "Agrippa becomes a very likely source indeed."

We have seen already how infinitely adaptable numbers are, and we have further illustrations here. Thus we learn (pp. 62–63) that Comus' first speech has "52 lines — the number of weeks in a year. Comus, in other words, presents himself as a representative of the sphere of mutability, of the realm of matter subjected to the rule of time" — just like, we might say, the Christian Platonist Henry Vaughan in the 52 lines of *Religion*, or *The Holy Communion*, or "Fair and yong light," or *The Men of War*. The second part of Comus' first speech (145–69), "where he prepares to cast his spell on the Lady, consists of 25 lines — the square of that number 5 which represents the world of sense" (p. 63). A parallel spokesman for the world of sense might be George Herbert, in the 25 lines (and not only that but 5 5-line stanzas) of *Unkindnesse* and *Aaron*. To return to *Comus*, the Lady's first speech (lines 170–229) has 60 lines, and 60 represents chastity, the perfect fulfillment of the law (pp. 64–65); for a 60-line poem that does not represent quite the same thing one might mention Thomas Randolph's *An Epithalamium*. Another item is probably unique and does not invite parallels. "The fact that Comus begins his great speech with line 666 — the notorious number of the beast in *Revelation* — is much too felicitous a circumstance to be the result of mere chance" (p. 67). One gathers that zealous readers of the early editions numbered all the lines in their copies to provide the material for brooding computation. However, unfortunate owners of the second edition of Milton's *Poems* (1673) would have missed the apocalyptic point, since in that edition — if they counted correctly — Comus' speech began at 665; for these readers too the second part of Comus' first speech would have had only 24 lines instead of the requisite 25. Other magical statistics we must pass over.

A century ago Matthew Arnold, deploring the extravagance and eccentricity of the provincial English mind, cited Renan's comment on the Charles Forster who had shown "that Mahomet was the little horn of the he-goat that figures in the eighth chapter of Daniel, and that the Pope was the great horn." In another essay he looked forward, not very hopefully, to a time when it might, "in English literature, be an objection to a proposition that it is absurd." That time seems farther off than ever. The learned and intuitive science of occult numbers is now becoming, or has already become, scholarly and highbrow orthodoxy. A generation ago almost any object on earth was a sexual symbol. Then came the army of myth-and-symbol exegetes, who enlarged the scope of imagination and found symbols of all kinds everywhere. With the latest phase we are completing a sort of cycle, since the examples considered here recall the ciphers and other underground operations of the Baconians and Oxfordians.

> Thy hand, great Anarch! lets the curtain fall,
> And universal Darkness buries All.

A Classical Scholar

On an afternoon a decade ago a rather unusual spectacle might have been observed on lower Yonge Street. Two figures emerged from Britnell's old bookshop and strode northward. I say "strode," but the word applies to only one of the two, a tall and more than substantial man of about sixty, with a full, ruddy face and bright blue eyes, who progressed with long and stately steps, *verus incessu patuit deus*. He carried his massive head a little on one side, and a small soft hat rode buoyantly on the waves of his white hair. His sober topcoat, restrained by only one button, floated behind him in the breeze; and while one hand rested in the small of his back the other rhythmically brandished a furled umbrella in the manner of Mr. Stokowski. Beside him a shorter and slighter young man of twenty kept more or less in step, by means of a stride alternated with a brief trot. The latter was saying nothing, having no breath anyhow, but he was listening ecstatically, for from the heights above him rolled a continuous stream of thunderous music. The older man, whose imagination was far away, and whose waving umbrella caused an occasional astonished pedestrian to leap off the curb, was chanting Kipling with royal gusto. On they went, the St. Bernard and the terrier, through

This sketch of Andrew J. Bell (1856–1932), Professor of Latin and Comparative Philology in the University of Toronto, appeared in *The Canadian Forum*, September 1929, and is reprinted by permission here. I am glad to remember that it gave him some pleasure.

Queen's Park, up to Avenue Road, and the glorious recital — from Kipling to Heine, Lucretius to Gautier — never ceased until the pair reached the old scholar's home.

That home had become a familiar place to the young man, a Zion where one could be happily at ease, and he knew how to thread his way dexterously over floors almost covered with tall piles of books which frequently tottered but by a miracle never fell. The two settled down in the study — there was still room to sit, for two — and talk began. In that room somehow talk never failed to lead, in five minutes or less, to Virgil and Horace. One crux after another was brought up, and tried on the dog, as it were. The young man was only becoming initiated into the subtleties of Latin style, but if his learning was slight his admiration and affection for his preceptor were infinite, and he was equally ready to share in the ceremonies as either junior priest or sacrificial victim. Leaning back in his capacious chair, his eyes shining with mirth and triumph, the old scholar would toss and gore Sidgwick and Page and Munro and Postgate. Those editors, they would never trust the manuscripts, they thought they knew more than Servius — if they read Servius — and they had that incurable disease, the *cacoethes emendendi!* Then he would dive into a corner for his first edition of Bentley's *Horace*, or perhaps some linguistic hare would be started, the verb "to be," say, in Umbrian and Oscan dialects, in Gothic, in the modern languages, with forays into Lithuanian and Old Norse. The young man would shiver slightly, for all his ecstasies, since he had been born without a trace of philological instinct.

But when the prey had been run to earth, and the young man's pallor perhaps become evident, that voice, which had stripped commentators to the bone, and chased vowels over Europe, would begin again to recite poetry. "Do you know so and so?" he would say. In the early days of their acquaintance the young man would eagerly answer "Yes," but he soon learned that "to know," to this man of Macaulayesque memory, meant "to know by heart," and he became more cautious. This was always the radiant part of the evening, when that voice, becoming warm, deep, sonorous, poured forth golden cadences. Sometimes he would reach for a book, and sometimes he would find it — happily for one's self-respect he did not know everything by heart — and the melodious chant would go on. Most people who recite poetry confirm one's habit of absorbing through the eye, but when this white-haired classic put on his singing-robes — to wit, carpet slippers and an old coat — a familiar poem became a new one.

And of course there was talk, roaming back and forth from Homer to Shaw, Virgil to Pepys, Scott, Chaucer, Burns, Rossetti, Balzac, Shakespeare. When the young man expressed opinions a sixty-year-old head was courteously inclined to receive them — to straighten up, perhaps, with a vigorous word of agreement, or vigorous but jovial dissent. Many old names were remembered, and saluted. To ardent youth there seemed nothing greater than scholars, and the life of the scholar, perpetual saturation in fine letters; surely in a lifetime one could pick up more than a few shells on the shore of the boundless ocean . . . The life so short, the craft so long to learn . . . Then a hand might fall suddenly upon one's knee, and upon one's ear the sound of an inward, reverberating chuckle which sought egress, and ended in "Scholar, my boy, does not rhyme with dollar." But the thud of descent to earth was softened by a gesture, at once complacent and modest, toward the walls, or the place where invisible walls presumably stood — "Still, I've been able to get a few books." Indeed, he had;

they numbered twenty-four thousand at the last count, and college tradition, for once authentic, told how a possible collapse of the house had necessitated the summoning of an engineer. "I have more incunabula than anyone in Canada," he went on, with that consciousness of achievement pardonable in epic heroes and book collectors of limited means. Unlike most book collectors, however, he had read his books; he knew all the literary (not to mention nonliterary) languages except Hebrew, and what human frailty the omission suggests he never avowed, though he did express the intention of mastering it shortly, and doubtless he has done so. "I know about as much English literature as the average professor of English," he once observed, and it was a prodigious understatement; his knowledge made one feel, in the words of George Eliot's villager, "no better nor a hollow stalk."

Then he might produce some Baxter prints, or some faded but precious letters, from the hands of Pitt, and Burns, and others. The latter name reminds one that perhaps nothing could have increased his devotion to Virgil except the discovery that he had been born in Scotland; in fact, when in the classroom he rendered the *Bucolics* into smoothly flowing English one had the feeling that in private he translated all the Virgilian plants and flowers into heather. Contemporary pacifism left him cold, or rather warm. "Rev. Dr. X," he exclaimed, "who ought to have known better, stood there and said nothing had ever really been won by battles. But," he sat up, gripping the arms of his chair with boyish glee, "I floored him with Bannockburn!"

How many generations of young men in that same room had seen visions and dreamed dreams! His home, he used to say (when the class had arrived at a certain spot in

Horace), did not need to be measured with a *decempeda*, a foot-rule would do — and there would follow that rumbling, heart-easing chuckle. But no four walls could contain more shadowy guests from the Elysian fields, and after such high converse with the mighty dead, young men left that house, in Horatian phrase, striking the stars with their exalted heads, wishing they could conquer all literature in one Gargantuan gulp. And the glow had not vanished before another invitation or chance meeting would come to renew it. Even Latin composition became a spiritual experience, and one could never be sure how far one's toil aimed at disinterested mastery of ancient idiom, how far at the not quite ignoble winning of an approving word from the master, who himself wrote as if his voluminous trailing gown were a toga made by Cicero's tailor.

How his mannerisms of speech and gesture were treasured in amused and reverent memory — that extended finger, rigid as a Roman javelin, which seemed to impale the luckless victim; that opening of the office door, precisely as the bell rang, then the slow advance, with head forward, and a little on one side, while the small group of students wished they had been somewhat more rigorous in preparation . . . The young man whose acquaintance has been sketched had occasional special shivers, for he seemed to be regularly called upon to translate the more doubtful bits of Catullus and other free-spoken ancients not appreciated by pre-war females . . .

He was not altogether a recluse. One day our young man met him near his home — it is to be feared that the young man sometimes strolled out of his way with certain possibilities in mind — and he walked with bent head and meditative mien, as if he had just come from the Library, or a meeting of the Caput. As a matter of fact he had just come from the Island, whither he had repaired by himself to witness a nonintellectual conflict between Toronto and Baltimore. And one of the most refreshing phrases in that austere work, *Who's Who*, lists under Recreations "Used to play golf." Nor can anyone who attended college social functions forget his elaborate old-fashioned courtesy toward the young women, who would rather have a greeting from him (along with a merry quip which bowled one over) than from their most dashing contemporaries. Now and then a brief excursus upon ancient Umbrian might disconcert a stranger, but after all is not a little Umbrian a pleasant change from the tedious small talk of receptions?

Like all men of learning and wisdom, he had, and has, some strong prejudices, though his most explosive utterances were generally accompanied by a twinkle of those keen blue eyes. Only one prejudice or conviction it was perhaps really dangerous to touch upon, and our young man never felt quite intimate enough to hazard the remark that some persons consider Latin inferior to Greek. University lore does indeed tell of a colleague who hinted at some such dark infamy, but the versions of his fate are so conflicting that possibly, as with some ancient heroes, a protecting deity carried him away in a mist. And it was just as well if one testified, early in conversation, to sound principles in the matter of the Latin dual.

He reminds one, in his single-hearted love of learning for its own sake and not for the sake of kudos, of some of the best Renaissance scholars. He has quietly gone his own way, without practicing or even understanding the arts of publicity, and the influence he has wielded for forty years has been almost wholly personal. Nor, like some famous academic characters, has he ever been a conscious influence, with an eye on the gallery. But simply by being himself he has made young men want to be like him. He reminds one, too, of a man who had no special Scottish sentiments, one Samuel Johnson, in his immense acquisitiveness, his honesty and sincerity, his downright and yet courtly manner, his devotion to literature, his freedom from all cant and humbug, his generous interest in aspiring youth, his stout prejudices and his hearty laughter. Such rich and mellow personalities have never been very numerous in universities — not so numerous in the past as sentimentalists like to think — and successors are hard to find. Meanwhile, scholars old and young, all over America, rekindle the memory of some of their happiest undergraduate hours when they think of that majestic figure, with one hand resting in the small of his back, still pacing through Queen's Park, murmuring (with a mental bow to Servius, that trusty guide), *Non ignara mali miseris succurrere disco.*

Bliss Perry

I FIRST SAT under Bliss Perry when I was a graduate student in the early 1920's, and found his courses a happy antidote to Gothic — though Mr. Perry never encouraged the rebellious emotions that surged up in many of us. And that reminds me of my oral examination. Orals used to begin with thirty or forty minutes of linguistics which seemed a hellish eternity to those without philological gifts, and after I had floundered for some time in a quicksand of Indo-European vowels and consonants, Mr. Perry quietly got up and stole out; I remember wondering, even in my dire straits, if his kind heart could not endure the scene any longer.

On the platform Mr. Perry was the same as he was in private. He had nothing of the showman about him; he didn't need to have. His bright blue eyes and his slow smile, at once amiable and quizzical, irradiated a warm and selfless concern with literature and with all things humane. The easy unpretentiousness of his manner now and then concealed, at the time, the shrewd and mellow wisdom of an apparently casual remark; but one would recall it afterwards and see that it had hit some nail on the head, or had deflated some fashionable cliché. Sometimes he would pause, his gaze turned inward for a moment, and we would know that an anecdote was coming. It might come from his wealth

Reprinted by permission from the *Harvard Alumni Bulletin*, November 25, 1950.

of reading, or from his wealth of literary friendships; sometimes it came from baseball, or fishing, or a hunting trip. But Mr. Perry did not feel apologetic in gliding from one realm to another, nor was he talking down to whatever boyishness might have lingered in his students; he was just being himself, savoring again some passages in a full and richly diversified life. I, having come from Canada with rather vague notions of the meaning of "New England" and "Yankee," soon decided that those traditions and flavors had simply been distilled in Bliss Perry.

In later times my wife and I had the happy fortune to be next-door neighbors to the Perrys, and we saw something of them almost daily for ten years, until they moved to Milton. One could not undertake to say in a few sentences, or in many, what such neighborly friendship meant, or what an abundance of memories remain fresh. I can see Mr. Perry on his knees digging out weeds, or emerging from his house to give our small son better instruction than mine on throwing a ball, or, beside his fire or ours, tapping his inexhaustible experience of letters and human nature. Listening to him often made one wish that *And Gladly Teach* — to mention only the most personal of his many books — had been twice as long as it is.

Mr. Perry's advice was so often sought by writers known and unknown, and so generously given, that he was sometimes in danger of being worn out by visitors who, fascinated by his talk, forgot that his body was not so vigorous as his mind. I trust I am not being indiscreet if I record that Mrs. Perry, who always had his welfare on her mind, made a private arrangement with me that, when she called up in terms of a simple code, I was to go over on pretense of urgent business and dislodge the visitor.

But one cannot get very far on paper in trying to suggest

the humanity, integrity, vitality, and charm of Bliss Perry, and I can only turn from random reminiscences to join happily in saluting him on his ninetieth birthday. And what it would be impertinent for me to say might perhaps be said, or partly said, in the words of Walter Pater, when Marius contemplates the Stoic professor, Fronto: "a perfectly tolerable, perfectly beautiful, old age — an old age in which there seemed . . . nothing to be regretted, nothing really lost, in what years had taken away. The wise old man, whose blue eyes and fair skin were so delicate, uncontaminate and clear, would seem to have replaced carefully and consciously each natural trait of youth, as it departed from him, by an equivalent grace of culture."

Arthur Woodhouse: Scholar, Critic, Humanist

When in my twenties I picked up a book dedicated by G. L. Kittredge to J. M. Manly, "my friend for almost thirty years," my involuntary thought was "What biblical patriarchs they both must be!" And now I can say "over forty years" about Arthur Woodhouse — if this were 1764, one would ejaculate *Eheu fugaces, Postume, Postume.* Though we were contemporaries at the University of Toronto, he was in Modern History at University College and I was in Classics at Victoria, so we did not meet until the spring of 1921, when we had both committed our destinies to the Harvard graduate school. In September we found ourselves in the queue of young men who had brief colloquies with Professor Kittredge as he sat on the porch steps of Warren House, immaculate and Olympian with white hair and beard and the invariable light-gray suit, boiled shirt, and cigar. I still remember the dampening of scholarly ardor that I felt when one young man in the queue asked another (later identified as Leslie Hotson and Thomas M. Raysor) if he was finishing that year and received the doleful answer "God willing." Arthur happened to follow me in the line and was later somewhat aggrieved

Reprinted by permission from *Essays in English Literature from the Renaissance to the Victorian Age Presented to A. S. P. Woodhouse, 1964*, ed. Millar MacLure and F. W. Watt (Toronto: University of Toronto Press, 1964). Arthur Woodhouse died suddenly on October 31, 1964 (some months after the presentation of this volume).

because I had sped smoothly through St. Peter's wicket while he had been held up on account of having acknowledged that he read German with a dictionary; I could only say, in all candor, that it had never occurred to me that anyone read German without a dictionary.

At that time the doctoral program of courses was a grim round of Gothic and kindred things, with bits of literature if they could be squeezed in. Those of us who were not philologically minded, the majority, led lives of quiet desperation relieved only on Saturday nights, when, like so many Typhons under Etna, we belched verbal lava, or sought escape in fifty-cent seats (or were they 25¢?) at a Boston repertory theatre. For those who craved more than dusty answers one positive and enduring relief was found in the courses of Irving Babbitt (I, unhappily, was then an ultra-romantic and would have none of him). Arthur recognized Babbitt's aesthetic and critical shortcomings and the degree of prejudice in his crusading zeal, but, like some other good minds, he, without being a blind disciple, valued such passionate concern with moral ideas that mattered.

In the 1920's the advanced study of literature, whether in doctoral theses or the most mature work, still meant chiefly "research" into sources, influences, literary backgrounds, a kind of study which had and has its solid virtues but, as commonly pursued, remained factual and external. Although the new historical study of ideas had been growing, it had not yet widely revitalized scholarship. Among thesis writers at Harvard and doubtless elsewhere there was subterranean rumbling against such limited endeavors, and Arthur and some others faced toward the new light. (He has never at any time been torn, as he once said of a troubled scholar, "between two slogans, 'Back to Saintsbury!' and 'On to the Records Office!' ")

Woodhouse — shifting from reminiscence to impersonal biography seems to require a shift from Christian name to surname, since one can't say "Professor" a hundred times — was well prepared both to resist Babbitt's erratic dogmatism and to absorb all that was good in him. As an undergraduate in University College he had matured under the sage and stable as well as stimulating wisdom and insight of such teachers as he later commemorated — W. J. Alexander, Malcolm Wallace, W. S. Milner, and others.[1] The very full and substantial account of Alexander as critic and teacher was written in 1944 by one "who, in simple truth, owes him everything." Allowing for Woodhouse's own natural growth, we may perhaps modify a phrase inspired by generous devotion and gratitude without underestimating his debt to Alexander's finely incisive, well-balanced, aesthetic, ethical, and political mind. Woodhouse's concentrating in history indicated his early bent and foreshadowed his lifelong concern not merely with religious and political thought but with the necessity of an historical approach to literature.

I embark on a short account of Woodhouse's studies in the history and interpretation of ideas with well-founded diffidence. When we were at Harvard together he was already showing his philosophical acumen and I was in the mental state represented by a remark of mine he did not allow me to forget — "I always knew that Locke was involved with innate ideas but I can never remember whether he was for them or against them" — an imbecility perhaps a little extenuated by struggles with Gothic and Middle English dialects but still not unrelated to congenital defects. So, as I say, I have misgivings. Besides, Woodhouse's expo-

[1] "In Memoriam: William John Alexander . . . II. Critic and Teacher," *University of Toronto Quarterly*, XIV (1944–45), 8–32; "Staff, 1890–1953," *University College: A Portrait*, ed. Claude T. Bissell (Toronto, 1953), pp. 51–83.

sitions are so carefully thought out and so carefully worded that brief summaries are hazardous as well as inadequate; and, finally, I cannot take account of his many reviews, which are never perfunctory but are themselves contributions to the subject in hand.

Woodhouse's first major publication was the elaborate "Collins and the Creative Imagination." [2] Here he spoke of Babbitt's having first aroused his interest in Romantic and pre-Romantic views of the creative imagination, but whatever the general stimulus of Babbitt and other teachers and of new approaches to the eighteenth century in scholarship at large, this monograph was a fresh, illuminating, and wholly disinterested inquiry. In analyzing and clarifying the pattern of eighteenth-century ideas and placing Collins' individual conception in that pattern, Woodhouse deployed much learning in the service of critical interpretation. The study showed what were to be characteristic qualities — clarity of thought and style and precise definition and discrimination, with nothing left loose or blurred.

Woodhouse's abiding interest in Romantic ideas — and in the whole philosophic pattern of the eighteenth and nineteenth centuries — has continued uninterruptedly in his teaching but has found public expression only in some reviews and in the paper, "Romanticism and the History of Ideas," read at the International Conference of University Professors of English held at Oxford in 1950.[3] This paper, printed in abridged form, was a further analysis of the role of the imagination in aesthetic theory from Sidney to Coleridge. It was a logical sequel to, or enlargement of, the study focused on Collins, and its philosophic range and

[2] *Studies in English by Members of University College, Toronto*, ed. Malcolm W. Wallace (Toronto, 1931), pp. 59–131.

[3] *English Studies Today*, ed. C. L. Wrenn and G. Bullough (New York, 1951), pp. 120–40.

density might suggest that the author, in the nineteen years between the two, had been reading nothing but British philosophy and aesthetics. He had, however, much earlier moved his center of gravity back to the seventeenth century, to its political and religious thought, and to the thought and poetry of Milton in particular. To this main line we may turn.

Woodhouse's shift coincided with early stirrings of modern inquiry in that troubled and exciting era. A number of scholars had been setting up "the new Milton" in opposition to the petrified image of the grim Puritan. In 1933–34 William Haller, Perry Miller, and a few others were bringing new documents and new light to the study of English and American Puritanism and were showing the complexity of a subject popularly assumed to be simple. (One remembers the classic capsule in *1066 and All That*: "The Royalists were wrong but romantic; the Roundheads were right but repulsive.") In a number of reviews and especially in the article "Milton, Puritanism, and Liberty,"[4] Woodhouse, already a master of the sources, set forth some seminal and more or less original ideas which he was to develop more fully in his later writings. One such idea was what he called the Puritan principle of segregation, the capacity, even of those who saw all life as enveloped by religion, to separate the secular from the religious — a principle at the center of problems of freedom of conscience, toleration, and the relations of church and state.

Still more central and important and, when Woodhouse began to expound and emphasize it, more novel was the doctrine of "Christian liberty," which Luther and Calvin had carried on from St. Paul and which for some seventeenth-century Englishmen, notably Milton, could become

[4] *University of Toronto Quarterly*, IV (1934–35), 483–518.

dynamic and revolutionary individualism. In brief, this meant the abolition of the Mosaic law, an involuntary and partly ceremonial code suitable for the early Jews' degree of enlightenment, and the Christian acceptance of free grace, the full freedom given to the regenerate through faith in Christ and the inward law of love. Woodhouse sees Milton's exposition of inward Christian liberty as presented wholly in ethical terms and the Miltonic state of grace as an ethical condition rather than a spiritual experience; this is certainly true for much of Milton, perhaps for all, but one may be inclined to qualify the judgment when one thinks of the peculiar elevation and intensity of Milton's ethical passion, of his almost mystical phrases about God and light and order, of the exultant passage on Christian liberty near the end of *Paradise Lost* (all of which, of course, Milton's interpreter knew and had weighed). In the public sphere, Woodhouse's comparison of Milton and Roger Williams in this article and elsewhere — a comparison writers on Williams do not always seem to have assimilated — illuminates both in showing how Milton's radicalism stopped short of the devoutly religious Williams' secular, egalitarian democracy; Milton the Renaissance humanist remained a classical republican, his "aristocratic" conception of the Platonic philosopher-king coalescing with the likewise "aristocratic" Puritan conception of "the saints."

Milton's was only one of many voices of the revolutionary era and Woodhouse's lecture of 1937 on "Puritanism and Democracy" [5] was a broader and fuller approximation to the introduction to *Puritanism and Liberty* and no less closely packed. In both, comprehensive and minute knowledge of the sources, controlled by discriminating insight,

[5] *Canadian Journal of Economics and Political Science*, IV (1938), 1–21.

enabled Woodhouse to chart a sea of theory and opinion so complex and confusing in the variations of individuals and groups that a less strong-minded and stout-hearted explorer might well despair of achieving any intelligible order. But Woodhouse is so saturated in the pamphlets and ideas of the period, in the mentality of persons and parties, that he can in a way think like them and then interpret their thinking in the light of a philosophic modern historian's understanding. Naturally he brushes aside the facile formulas about Puritan "rationalizations" that find such ready acceptance among secular liberals who cannot comprehend religious motives. Instead, Woodhouse demonstrates how the central and constant vision of "the holy community" could inspire the most complex diversities in religious and political thought, and how logical apparent inconsistencies turn out to be. In this article there is further development of concepts that Woodhouse has made his own, Christian liberty, the principle of segregation, and — appearing perhaps for the first time — another version of the latter, "the dogma of the two orders," that is, nature and grace. This phrase, a larger and more suggestive formulation, is to furnish the key for later interpretations of poetry.

Puritanism and Liberty (1938; second edition, 1950) was recognized at once as a standard book, indispensable for anyone who would understand seventeenth-century Puritan thought, religious and political. While the texts reprinted are mainly those of the Army Debates of 1647–1649 on the constitutional settlement, the twin questions of political democracy and religious liberty, the spectrum is filled out with supplementary extracts carefully selected. In the controversial confusion after the civil war the large pattern of victorious Puritanism shows reactionary Presbyterianism on the right, liberal and progressive Independency in the center, and miscellaneous radical sects and parties on the left; and, apart from all these, is a loose group of secular Erastians. But within this general pattern and within parties, as we have noted already, there were endless variations; everyone who had the gift of utterance (and few men lacked it) had his own thoughts or visions to proclaim. In the ninety-page introduction the main attitudes and ideas treated in Woodhouse's earlier articles naturally reappear, now further developed and set in a fuller context. All the general and some particular comments that were made on the articles may be emphasized and enlarged in their application to this work. The author's immediate task, a sufficiently difficult one, is to interpret the Army Debates and place them in their setting; but the introduction goes far beyond that and is, in fact, the most compendious, fully rounded, and closely discriminating analysis we have of mid-century Puritan beliefs, ideas, and modes of thought. In spite of the lucidity of the exposition, its specific gravity is so high that — to change metaphors — digestion requires more than one or two readings.

Woodhouse's chief later discussion of political thought was "Religion and Some Foundations of English Democracy,"[6] in which the Puritans were overshadowed by Hooker — a figure in himself more congenial to Woodhouse's Anglican temper and strong sympathy with the tradition of Christian humanism. Apart from this, the paper on Romanticism already noticed, discussions of the humanities at large or in Canada, and several reviews, his writings in the last dozen years have been mainly Miltonic and mainly literary. One of these is of more scholarly than critical concern (though the distinction, in regard to Milton, is only relative). "Notes on Milton's Views on the

[6] *Philosophical Review*, LXI (1952), 503–31.

Creation: The Initial Phases"[7] dealt with Milton's heretical view of the creation as *de Deo*, not *ex nihilo*, and with the striking religious and metaphysical implications of that doctrine. The very full "Notes on Milton's Early Development"[8] is also of mainly scholarly concern, although Woodhouse uses Milton's ideas and attitudes along with external evidence in his attempt to date and arrange in sequence a number of Milton's early poems and thus make coherent a partly cloudy phase of his poetic evolution. The weighing of imponderables and inferences drawn therefrom are necessarily tentative, but there are here, along with critical comments on Latin and English poems, some persuasive arguments which have somehow been neglected by scholars pursuing the same problems.

Discussing "practical criticism" with special reference to Milton,[9] Woodhouse laid down a simple and judicious principle: "The business of the critic of poetry is with the understanding and appreciation of individual poems and of a poet's total output as expressive of his mind." Understanding and appreciation "are mutually dependent," but the former stresses historical knowledge and relative objectivity, while the latter is inevitably more subjective. Woodhouse's approach to Milton's poetry is mainly historical, but it issues in the most substantial kind of appreciation. The first and probably the best-known and most discussed of his Miltonic critiques was "The Argument of Milton's *Comus*,"[10] which has been pronounced "within

[7] *Philological Quarterly*, XXVIII (1949), 211–36.

[8] *University of Toronto Quarterly*, XIII (1942–43), 66–101.

[9] "The Approach to Milton: A Note on Practical Criticism," *Transactions of the Royal Society of Canada*, Third Series, XXXVIII (1944), section II, 201–13. A later extension was "The Historical Criticism of Milton," *PMLA*, LXVI (1951), 1033–44.

[10] *University of Toronto Quarterly*, XI (1941–42), 46–71; supplemented by "*Comus* Once More," ibid., XIX (1949–50), 218–23.

the limits of its defined purpose, the best study of the poem we know, the only commentary we could recommend as an indispensable aid to the reading of *Comus*,"[11] and "the most seminal influence on Milton criticism since Tillyard's *Milton* in 1930."[12] The essay is a cardinal example of the necessity and value of historical criticism, of setting forth a poet's assumptions, his intellectual frame of reference, which in his own time he could take for granted but which must be rebuilt for modern readers. Here that frame of reference is what Woodhouse had already designated as "the dogma of the two orders" of nature and grace. These two orders had been a primary fact of consciousness throughout the Christian tradition; no educated person could be unaware of the gulf between the natural light of pagan reason and the illumination of Christian truth, a gulf which Christian humanists had always tried to bridge by making pagan reason and the rational pagan virtues stepping stones to Christian virtue and faith. But, however familiar this general tradition, Woodhouse was the first to formulate it in full, explicit, and usable terms and apply it directly to *Comus*. (Milton himself, in the *Apology for Smectymnuus* of 1642, was quite open in relating "the noblest philosophy" of the pagans, Plato above all, to Christian teaching.) Woodhouse sees in *Comus* a triple equation: temperance or continence, which belongs to the order of nature; chastity, which is grounded in nature but, in Platonic terms, approaches the level of grace; and virginity, the illustration and symbol of purely Christian grace. Some readers find this scheme more elaborate and specific than Milton's text

[11] Cleanth Brooks and J. E. Hardy, *Poems of Mr. John Milton* (New York, 1951), pp. 235–36.

[12] W. G. Madsen, "The Idea of Nature in Milton's Poetry," *Three Studies in the Renaissance: Sidney, Jonson, Milton*, by R. B. Young, W. T. Furniss, and W. G. Madsen (New Haven, 1958), p. 214.

seems to warrant and would ask if he makes a clear distinction between chastity and virginity. However, even with such a possible reservation the essay loses little of its enlightening quality. Since it is so well known, one need not attempt a summary — and, as I remarked before, it is hard to summarize Woodhouse's closely wrought expositions. Among other things, he completely extinguishes the not uncommon notion that Milton's conception of chastity, of virtue, was austerely negative; on the contrary, it was positive and glowing. A more special point is the first explicit interpretation of the difficult epilogue. Another special point was added in a later note, the idea that Sabrina is a symbol of grace. This is a brilliantly logical intuition and certainly what Milton should have meant, though one may not feel quite sure that he did mean that, since the chief local legend provided a graceful ending and since Sabrina is enveloped in mythological reference to a degree rather beyond even the large freedom of Christian poetry of the Renaissance. But perhaps such objections are not strong enough to stand against so persuasive a suggestion.

The theme of this article and references in it to Spenser invite us to digress from the Miltonic path and take in a Johns Hopkins lecture of 1949, "Nature and Grace in *The Faerie Queene*."[13] For Spenser, as for Milton and other men, the dual order was a central and all-embracing fact, and he himself had signalized both the difference and the measure of affinity by making Holiness and Temperance the themes of the partly parallel narratives of his first two books. In interpreting Spenser's conception and delineation of the Christian and classical orders and virtues, Woodhouse shows his usual concern for precise definition, since essential points may not be manifest to modern readers

[13] *ELH*, XVI (1949), 194–228.

unversed in theology. Thus when Arthur rescues the Red Cross Knight from Orgoglio's dungeon, the act signifies the infusion of grace into the will of the sinner; when, however, Arthur protects the prostrate Guyon from enemies, he represents, not grace, but magnanimity (his normal role) and also the intervention of Providence in the natural order. One new, brilliant, and wholly convincing idea is that the diseased, grisly, and almost invincible Maleger, captain of the band attacking the house of Alma (mind and body), symbolizes original sin; his strength is renewed by contact with earth, and he is destroyed only when cast into the water (of baptism). Since all fresh and good criticism provokes queries, one may question Woodhouse's putting his thesis or hypothesis as a complete dichotomy: that grace operates only in book one, nature (sometimes with Providence as ally) everywhere else. His own interpretation of Maleger, a figure in the book of classical temperance, makes one admitted and striking exception, and there may be one or two other arguable cases, such as Britomart. But, even if one hesitates over a few particulars, the study has the great value of providing a point of view that clarifies and enriches our reading of Spenser and adds dimensions and subtleties that we might easily miss.

To return to Milton, in "Milton's Pastoral Monodies" [14] Woodhouse treated two poems in which Milton characteristically focused "upon the drama of his own existence," both representative of his double inheritance, classical and Christian. In the relatively impersonal *Lycidas* and the directly personal *Epitaphium Damonis*, as in *Comus* and indeed all Milton's major poems, experience poses a problem "demanding to be either solved or transcended" and

[14] *Studies in Honour of Gilbert Norwood* (Toronto, 1952), pp. 261–78.

generating "an emotional tension requiring to be resolved." And in both elegies Milton employed what the pastoral tradition fully sanctioned, "a species of allegory which is midway between direct statement and dramatic projection." The account of *Lycidas*, though short, is one of the best-rounded discussions of that complex and much-discussed poem, notably of its mingled classical and Christian strains. But the explication of the *Epitaphium*, probably the fullest and freshest the poem has ever had, is more provocative. Woodhouse's subtle analysis of structure, texture, and symbolism almost convinces me that the *Epitaphium* is a much better poem than I am able to think it is.

Woodhouse's central concern with theme and structure is in tacit opposition to the recent tendency to emphasize imagery at the cost of more basic elements. This concern governs his essays on the three late and long works. In "The Pattern of *Paradise Lost*" [15] he starts as usual from firm and familiar ground, in this case the premise that "Milton's principal models were Homer and Virgil, and that what he was attempting was a classical epic poem on a Christian subject." But Woodhouse does not take the commonplace road. He illustrates Milton's sense of design in two microcosmic passages — Eve's asseveration of her love for Adam (iv.634–58) and the invocation to Light (iii.1–55) — and goes on to the design of the whole and to thematic and structural comparisons with the ancient epics. Here again the orders of nature and grace serve as a basis. Since Milton's theme is Christian, his poem is a divine comedy, though with "ample provision for tragic episodes." In his conception of Providence and in his structural pattern Milton is closer to Virgil than to Homer — and also in the prophetic pictures of human history in books xi–xii, even if, as individ-

[15] *University of Toronto Quarterly*, XXII (1952–53), 109–27.

ual pictures, they resemble those on the shield of Achilles. *Paradise Lost* has two protagonists, the earthly Adam and the heavenly Christ, who redeems what Adam lost. As for Satan, Milton does not abandon "the pagan standard of the heroic"; "in Satan it is presented, judged, and condemned." The poem as a whole is true to its title in concentrating upon the fall of man, not his recovery, though it ends on the note of "peace with hope."

Coming to *Paradise Regained*,[16] Woodhouse aims as usual at the center of the target and his essay is a pretty complete guide to the reading of this shorter poem. He feels no need of defending a work that has been relatively disparaged ever since it was published, and his assumptions concerning its very Miltonic power are quietly borne out by fresh comment on theme, structure, and some significant details. One example of pregnant succinctness is his summary of the climactic temptation, which resolves the dramatic tension of the whole by revealing Christ's true identity to both Satan and himself:

> Satan's intention is that Christ shall fall and the result will answer his question. His injunction to stand is purely ironical: that it is possible, he never for a moment conceives. But if Satan can be ironical, so can Christ and the event. For the first and only time, he complies with Satan's suggestion; but it is not in surrender to Satan: it is in obedience to God— like Samson's going to the festival of Dagon. This is Christ's supreme act of obedience and trust, and it is also the long-awaited demonstration of divinity. The poem's two themes are finally and securely united; and "Tempt not the Lord thy God" carries a double meaning, for, in addition to its immediate application, it is Christ's first claim to participate in the Godhead. In an instant, and by the same event, Satan receives his answer and Christ achieves full knowledge of himself.

[16] "Theme and Pattern in *Paradise Regained*," *University of Toronto Quarterly*, XXV (1955–56), 167–82.

Two essays on *Samson Agonistes*, of 1949 and 1958, go together and their titles indicate their respective emphasis.[17] Woodhouse would date the tragedy in 1660–61, as against both the traditional 1667–1670 and the recent (and surely quite untenable) arguments for 1646–1648 or 1652–53. His reasons are that Milton's personal experience in 1660–61 would best explain the mood of *Samson*, which is out of key with the settled equanimity of his later years, and that that date would make acceptable what seem to be clear topical and personal allusions; Woodhouse concedes that the drama might have sprung from a later temporary depression and might therefore be what conventional opinion has made it, Milton's last work (which seems to me a somewhat preferable view). In any case the drama links itself with the two epics in its theme of "temptation, disobedience, repentance, obedience, restoration," though here "the whole series is run through in the person of the hero." All three works are assertions of eternal Providence, and when Milton composed *Samson* such an assertion would test even his invincible faith. In the first essay Woodhouse considers the degree to which Milton's experience is projected and sublimated in the drama — not that he set out on dramatic autobiography but that his chosen theme kindled and was kindled by thoughts of his nation's and his own heroic past and of the ignoble Restoration. Woodhouse, with conscious temerity, suggests that Samson's sin and confession of sin reflect Milton's retrospective view of his own disastrous first marriage.

Remarks in the first essay on *Samson* as a Christian tragedy in Greek form are enlarged in the second. Some critics

[17] "*Samson Agonistes* and Milton's Experience," *Transactions of the Royal Society of Canada*, Third Series, XLIII (1949), section II, 157–75; "Tragic Effect in *Samson Agonistes*," *University of Toronto Quarterly*, XXVIII (1958–59), 205–22.

have denied the general possibility of a Christian tragedy because faith in Providence or in heaven would rule that out; but Woodhouse makes clear how such faith can accommodate what are, in a limited human view, tragic events. "If he [Samson] is an instrument of Providence, he does not cease to be an individual, fallible, though corrigible, heroic — and by his own action doomed." Milton works on the human level before invoking the providential, and in this Hebraic drama he does not invoke any hope of heaven. Samson and Hamlet alike perish at last in giving effect to the moral order. "They are on the side of the power — the overruling power — which destroys them." Milton "has made the way of repentance and restoration, the way back to God, also the way that leads inevitably to the catastrophe, and has thus achieved at a stroke the only kind of irony that is at once compatible with a Christian outlook and as potent as any to be found in tragedy anywhere."

Attitudes and ideas assumed or expounded throughout these Miltonic essays are drawn together in the first Sedgewick Memorial Lecture, "Milton the Poet," delivered at the University of British Columbia in 1955.[18] Perhaps the most basic premise of all Woodhouse's Miltonic criticism is the unity of Milton's personal, aesthetic, and religious experience. Some general facts and ideas summarized in this lecture are: Milton's "strong sense of literary tradition and of genre"; his originality, which re-creates traditional forms; his feeling for aesthetic pattern and for what that is woven upon, "a firm structural framework" (and these are not static but dynamic and progressive). A more general principle, of a poem as the realization of experience, holds for any poet, but for Milton in a special way as condi-

[18] Published as a pamphlet by Dent (Toronto, 1955).

tioned by the instincts and gifts already indicated: an "extraesthetic experience, problematic and productive of tension," is objectified in a poem but reviewed "in the light of the poet's profounder convictions, which likewise receive poetic utterance; and the result is the transcending of the problem. But both steps are taken under the impetus of an aesthetic pattern; and it is not enough to say that the problem is transcended: the emotional tension is also resolved." Woodhouse then goes on to analyze the various workings of such principles in Milton's poems. Ideas that we have met before are compressed into a compendious whole; they can be because they have developed so coherently in the critic's mind — a process brought home to one by the consecutive rereading of the whole series of essays. The lecture is thus a "short view" of the results of Woodhouse's long and penetrating study of Milton and his age. It is also of special interest because its opening is a statement of his own position in respect to current critical fashions — a statement enlivened by the urbane and incisive wit that sprinkles Attic salt and pepper over his conversation.

It might be wished that these Miltonic essays had been collected long ago, and one may still hope; at any rate Woodhouse will be discussing and annotating all the minor poems in the Variorum Commentary that is in prospect. One volume that will doubtless soon appear, and will take in Spenser and Milton and much else, I can only refer to — the Weil Institute lectures.[19]

Woodhouse's long and large services, in action and in print, to the study of the humanities in Canada would demand another paper. This rapid and most inadequate

[19] Posthumously published as *The Poet and his Faith: Religion and Poetry in England from Spenser to Eliot and Auden* (Chicago, 1965).

survey of his writings on history and literature cannot begin to suggest how much he has taught students of all ages on several continents. He has been equally strong as an historical analyst of ideas and as a critic of poetry, and these two faculties, not often found together, have strengthened each other. His writings combine active learning, philosophic breadth and depth, and aesthetic insight — both "wit" and "judgment," in the old sense, in a rare and happy balance — and these virtues are all fructified and warmed by an understanding of Milton in particular that is at once profoundly sympathetic and wholly candid.

The qualities of mind and character that are the strength of Woodhouse's writings are no less, it may be assumed, the strength of his classroom teaching. In two general discourses on the humanities he started, characteristically, from history and worked up to the elements of both continuity and change in the modern study of literature.[20] Characteristic also was his refusal to leave the plane of sober fact and dispassionate thought for emotional and inspirational rhapsody. It is not, he affirms, the function of a humanist to indoctrinate, to try to spiritualize the community, but to expound his authors as best he can and let their art and wisdom do their own work. Among the major groups of disciplines only the humanities have as their "sole purpose the general cultivation of mind and sensibility which was the traditional end of liberal education." The writings of Arthur Woodhouse achieve that end.

[20] "The Nature and Function of the Humanities," *Transactions of the Royal Society of Canada*, Third Series, XLVI (1952), section II, 1–17; "The Place of Literature in the Humanities," *Man and Learning in Modern Society* (Seattle, 1959), pp. 111–25.

T. S. Eliot

T. S. ELIOT WAS born in 1888, some months after Matthew Arnold died, and I once suggested a possible transmigration of souls. Mr. Eliot himself might not have fully relished this fancy (although in his later years, in conversation at least, he had somewhat mellowed toward Arnold), but it is one of the obvious facts of modern literary history that he inherited Arnold's dual role as poet and critic. Since for him these roles were concurrent, not consecutive, he reached, at an earlier age than Arnold, a position of much stronger authority than Arnold's among the literary in England and the United States; and he was widely read and translated in foreign countries. Through a whole generation Mr. Eliot was the quiet dictator of critical ideas and literary taste. His most casual phrases — if his phrases ever were casual — became oracular.

The two reasons were of course his poetry and his prose. His radically original genius made him the leader of the modern movement in poetry, and his critical essays, directly or indirectly, explained and guided and defended that movement. At first he seemed, like the John Donne whom he had read at Harvard and whose modern vogue he helped greatly to promote, to be a rebel against the supposedly effete tradition of romanticism. As that revolt recedes into history, it may look less like classicism than like

Read at the memorial service in the Harvard Memorial Church, January 20, 1965.

a new kind of romanticism — and at Harvard Eliot had also been steeped in nineteenth-century poetry, English and French. At any rate, when in 1928 he declared himself a classicist, a royalist, and an Anglo-Catholic, these labels — if they disconcerted or dismayed a number of good liberals — were reminders that, as both poet and critic, Eliot was not merely an individual but the voice of tradition. Like Arnold, he was a very conscious spokesman for cosmopolitan culture and for all literature as a body of organic wholes. Thus, whatever his idiosyncrasies, he was never simply a great poet or a great critic but an institution, a kind of French Academy in himself.

Although his first poems, with their learned, elliptical wit, caused much bewilderment, Mr. Eliot taught his age to enjoy an ultra-modern mode, and for many years he had, we may suppose, the satisfaction of knowing himself a secure classic — even a classic to be rebelled against. It is idle to indulge in prophecies, but we may guess that his late plays will retain some interest because they were his and were experimental efforts to put religious ideas into popular form; that — to continue with prophecy — his criticism (if its lucid elegance is not a fatal handicap in an age of increasing jargon) will live chiefly as an historical guide to a period and a biographical guide to his own poetic aims and outlook; and that what will continue to be cherished entirely for its own sake will be his nondramatic poetry. He left no bad work to be lopped off; what he wrote is a firm and shapely corpus. It is all the more firm because, beginning with *Prufrock*, it embodies a steady evolution, from penetrating satire to mystical meditation. *The Waste Land* was Mr. Eliot's *Inferno*, *Ash Wednesday* his *Purgatorio*, and *Four Quartets* his *Paradiso*. The early Eliot, like the early Arnold, turned from an ugly present to an ideal mythic past; the later Eliot, unlike Arnold, moved from the diagnosis of spiritual squalor to a vision in which the fire and the rose are one. It might have seemed impossible that, in our day, such eminence and influence as his could have been attained by a Christian poet; yet, in a time of disorder, a sober quest for order may be exciting and compelling, and even readers unsympathetic toward the poet's creed can hardly resist his magical power of image and phrase and rhythm or deny the value and beauty of the experience he distilled.

Tudor Humanism and Henry VIII

In his admirable *Thomas More*, Professor R. W. Chambers pillories Henry VIII as the ruthless destroyer of the rich culture which England possessed at the opening of the sixteenth century. He makes his own the argument put forth by J. S. Phillimore [1] in what he calls "a vital essay, to which every student of More is under a heavy debt." Phillimore's thesis was "that the Humanist Movement in England was arrested at the middle of the sixteenth century and did not mature till more than a century later; that the movement was typically personified in More; and that his death was the blow which paralysed it." Mr. Chambers elaborates "the story of arrest and frustration" in this manner:

> The poets flocked to Henry's court; he stopped their music, and for a generation after the execution of Surrey there is nothing worth notice, save the sombre poems in which Sackville, before turning away from poetry, lamented that eminence led only to destruction. In the ordinary course, Surrey might have lived another thirty or forty years, the centre of a circle of court poets. As it is, the history of the sonnet in England is a blank between 1547 and about 1580, and English poetry as a whole is negligible till it begins its magnificent progress again with Spenser and Sidney. Prose had a similar set-back. After the generation of Tyndale and Coverdale, Fisher and More and his school, there is no eminence till we come to Hooker and Bacon — a gap of more than a genera-

Reprinted by permission from the *University of Toronto Quarterly*, January 1938.

[1] *Dublin Review*, 1913.

tion. Contemporaries noticed the gap, and wondered that More's example had not proved more fruitful. In the field of scholarship Henry's achievement was really remarkable. There were four great international scholars, and, in England, two great patrons of learning. Of the six, Henry cold-shouldered Erasmus out of England, imprisoned Vives, decapitated More and Fisher, and frightened Wolsey to death. "Had Erasmus, instead of being an honoured guest at Rome, at Paris, or in the States of the Empire, been beheaded by Charles V or Francis I, all learning would have felt the blow, and shrunk." [2] In England, all learning felt the blow, and shrank. It was not till the days of Bentley that classical scholarship recovered in England the position it held in the days of Erasmus, before Henry axed it. To the Universities, Henry's spoliation meant a loss, for which the foundation of a few Readerships offered small compensation. In 1550 Latimer writes, "It would pity a man's heart to hear that, that I hear of the state of Cambridge. . . . I think there be at this day ten thousand students less than were within these twenty years, and fewer preachers." As to the grammar schools, More's school of St. Antony was only one of a vast number which withered away.[3]

In a brief survey of a complex problem I must pass by many topics that Mr. Chambers touches. The lack of good poets in the middle of the century, for instance, might be charged against God rather than against his royal representative, for there are many ages of peace and plenty in which good poets simply do not happen to be born. As for a blank in the history of the sonnet between 1547 and 1580, if Henry was responsible for that it ought to be listed along with the royal navy as one of his major achievements; one could almost wish that the blank had continued. And, in spite of Mr. Chambers' notable study of early English prose, one is bewildered by the critical judgment which

[2] Phillimore.

[3] *Thomas More* (London, 1935), p. 379. In his new book, *The Place of Saint Thomas More in English Literature and History* (London, 1937), Professor Chambers returns to the charge (e.g., pp. 79, 92ff), but I find no occasion to modify anything I have said.

finds no eminence in prose between More's time and Hooker and Bacon. Is there no eminence in the *Book of Common Prayer*, in North's *Plutarch*, in Sidney's *Defence of Poesy*, in Hakluyt's *Voyages*, not to mention such lesser but able prosemen as Ascham, Hoby, Richard Eden, and others?

But our concern here is with humanism in its special sense, and with the theory that it was paralyzed by the execution of More. The proponents of this view give small evidence that the execution of the lord chancellor of England was felt as a blow to learning; they only feel that that must have been the effect. But, granted for the moment that the arrest of humanism was as complete as these scholars allege, there were far too many factors involved to permit any such simple explanation. I cannot find reason to suppose that the course of Tudor humanism would have been very different from what it was if More and Fisher had never been executed. To say that is not, of course, to slight the great service that both men, especially Fisher, did to learning.

For the main cause of the setback to learning in the universities, one has only to recall the conditions in which scholars were living. In the twenty-five years from 1535 to 1560 the official religion of the country changed four times, from papal to non-papal Catholicism, from that to Protestantism, from Protestantism to papal Catholicism, and from that to Protestantism again. The university men who lived through this period were, of course, at the center of religious and political controversy and were subjected, directly or indirectly, to successive and conflicting religious tests. And no sooner had the Elizabethan settlement been reached than strife between Anglican and Puritan commenced. From looking abroad at the present time we know how difficult it is for disinterested learning to flourish when scholars have lost their consciousness of freedom and security. In the middle of the sixteenth century there were keener anxieties than that — the fear of eating mice at Zürich, or, much worse, of imprisonment and death. Ascham, thanks largely to the Catholic Gardiner, weathered the storms, but he had some unhappy years. Cheke ended his life miserably with exile, imprisonment, and recantation. Henry VIII was responsible for only the beginning of these troubles, and the later burning of Latimer, Ridley, and Cranmer at Oxford may appear to have been a much greater and more direct blow to learning than the execution of More. Apart from such eminent victims, the history of most of the colleges throughout the period reveals continual disturbance and continual changing of masters, according as the reforming or the conservative party got the upper hand. And there was a vast amount of ecclesiastical controversy, ranging from Henry' divorce to the Eucharist. Amid such unrest, such vicissitudes, and such polemics, the wonder is that humanism did not suffer far more than it did.

Modern writers often assign as a major cause for the decline of the universities and of education in general the dissolution of the monasteries and along with them of monastic schools. Much of the mist of sentimental nostalgia and prejudice which has clung about that business has been dispelled by a number of recent historians. The latest of these, Mr. Geoffrey Baskerville, has shown that a long overdue process of nationalization was carried out in a remarkably careful and equitable manner, with remarkably generous provision for dispossessed monks and nuns. While Mr. Baskerville has not much to say about the effect of the dissolution on education, his verdict is that the effect was small, since monastic educational effort had long been declining. The dispersal of monastic libraries is a lamentable fact which does not concern us here, but something can be said of the relation between the monasteries and the schools and universities.

Medieval statutes required monastic houses to keep a teacher to instruct the monks in grammar, logic, and philosophy, and to send one out of every twenty monks to a university to learn theology or canon law. It does not appear that these rules were very effectively observed, at least in the period under discussion. In his visitation of so important a center as Canterbury, in 1511, Archbishop Warham complained of the lack of a teacher and of the monks' ignorance of even the services. The general evidence of monastic laxity gives small ground for such a statement as that of Mullinger, the historian of Cambridge, that the dissolution, in cutting off the supply of students from the monasteries, must have caused a temporary diminution in numbers at the universities "scarcely less serious than would result, in the present day, from a sudden diversion of those educated at the public schools." Such an estimate, indeed, is scarcely borne out by the facts and figures in Mullinger's own pages.

The dissolution no doubt had its indirect consequences. Scholars were afraid that the universities would follow the monasteries. But when in 1545 the act for the dissolution of the colleges was passed, the royal commissioners, through the contrivance of Sir Thomas Smith, were chosen from among university men. On receiving their report, says Matthew Parker, the king diligently perused it, and then "in a certen admiration saide to certen of his Lords which stode by that he thought he had not in his realme so many persons so honestly mayntayned in lyvyng bi so little lond and rent." Accordingly, instead of dissolving the colleges, Henry endowed the splendid foundation of Trinity College, Cambridge, an embodiment of the new learning whose chief men were drawn from that nursery of humanism, St. John's. A decade earlier Henry had begun the refoundation of Wolsey's Cardinal College. The king is often blamed both for not using monastic funds for college endowments and for using them. At any rate his chief immediate precedents for building colleges out of confiscated abbeys were furnished by those patrons of learning whom Mr. Chambers rightly admires, the saintly Fisher and the less saintly Wolsey. And one might add William of Wykeham and William of Wayneflete, for in fact Henry was only doing on a large scale what had been done for ages on a small one.

The dissolution is also commonly said to have injured education by destroying schools. We might recall Mr. Chambers' remark, one of his many charges against Henry, that More's school of St. Antony "was only one of a vast number which withered away." Mr. Chambers may be said to take a long view; St. Antony's School did wither away — in the middle of the seventeenth century. Since it is impossible to go into detail about schools, I must fall back on A. F. Leach, whose lifetime of research made his work so solid that subsequent writers have not found much to alter. I cite Leach not only because of his general authority, but because long study modified his own view of Henry. In his first book, *English Schools at the Reformation* (1896), he was not too friendly to the king. In his last book, *The Schools of Medieval England* (1915), he was led to such general judgments as these:

> Henry VIII's chief work in education consisted in refoundation and improvement, not in creation of new schools, but he did it on

a scale which entitles him to the praise of being, in a sense, the greatest of school founders.

It has been commonly assumed that in abolishing the monasteries he abolished a large number of schools. . . . This assumption is founded on the erroneous notion that the monasteries were or kept schools. . . .

The schools which Henry abolished in abolishing the monasteries were the small and insignificant almonry schools of a few charity boys, and these he more than replaced by the great schools which he established in the new cathedral foundations.

The abolition of the greater monasteries in 1540 resulted in the refoundation of twelve grammar schools as part of the cathedrals "of the new foundation" . . . . In all the new cathedrals established in 1541 . . . a grammar school, with a master and usher paid on the highest scale of the day, was included. . . .

The Schools thus refounded did the greater part of the education of England till the eighteenth century.

While some of these cathedral schools may not have got actively under way in Henry's time, the main facts stand. He doubtless would have done more still if the expenses of war had not come first. This advance in secondary education under Henry would have gone further in the next reign if the avowed intention of the early acts of Edward's Council had been carried out. First, all chantry priests were ordered to exercise themselves in teaching the young. This subsidiary duty of the numerous chantry priests had been much neglected, and individual bishops, such as Hugh Latimer, had already issued diocesan injunctions about it. Then the lands of chantries were taken over with the object of promoting education and charity in addition to eradicating Roman Catholicism. But money was needed for war with Scotland, chantry lands were sold, and many schools, left unprovided for, disappeared. It is to be observed that the chief contemporary laments come in and around 1550, from such divines as

Lever, Latimer, and Becon. These men, though vigorous Protestants, seem to be thinking of Edward's time and of Edward's rapacious courtiers rather than of Henry's. But even these laments, as we shall see, convict themselves of rhetorical excess.

The names of Latimer and Lever remind us of another cause of a fall in enrollment at the universities. Hitherto, says Latimer in 1549–50, the universities had been open to poor men's sons like himself, but the great increase in rents has crippled the yeoman class and limited higher education to the sons of the wealthy. On the other hand, the middle and upper classes were growing richer, and both the newly rich and the old aristocratic families saw the attractions of the universities for their sons. There is a good deal of testimony from such men as Latimer, Lever, Walter Haddon, Ascham, Caius, and William Harrison, about the decrease in poor and industrious students and the increase in wealthy idlers. Yet again we must allow for the academic instinct to regret the good old times. When we look back to those times we find, for instance, that many middle-aged priests had been deserting their parishes in order to enjoy the tavern side of college life; an Act of 1536 compelled all over forty to return to their cures, and those under forty to give proof of diligence in study. As for the increasing number of wealthy idlers who did not take degrees, we know that, during the first years of Elizabeth at least, the number of students at Cambridge was increasing very rapidly, but the proportion of B.A. degrees was increasing more rapidly still.

After laming ourselves with reasons we might wonder that the universities were still existing at all. But the depression does not seem to have been so serious as early and modern commentators have said it was. By telescoping bits from different sermons Mr. Chambers makes Latimer in

1550 appear to report ten thousand fewer students at Cambridge than there had been twenty years before. Latimer does not name any institution when he gives the figure of ten thousand, and if he had Cambridge in mind he was using very round numbers indeed; in 1564, when the registration had been rising for years, the total number of students at Cambridge was 1,267. What Latimer is always deploring is the falling-off in divinity students. At Cambridge in 1549–1551 there were two doctors of divinity and fourteen bachelors; twenty years before, in 1529–1531, there had been eleven of each. The decline does not seem overwhelming. In degrees of all kinds, the number fell from an average of 93 during 1522–1533 to an average of 78 in the next decade. Mullinger puts the greatest depression at both universities in the years 1542–1548; yet at the beginning of that period we have Ascham rejoicing in a golden age at Cambridge, and at the end of it we have Walter Haddon declaring that he had never seen the university more affluent or more thronged. And Mullinger admits that during those six dark years the number of B.A. degrees was only slightly smaller than during the six years of Edward's reign. Further, unfortunately for those who make Mary's reign the dark era, the number of B.A.'s during her five years was 195, compared with 167 during the last five years of Edward. At Oxford, according to Sir Charles Mallet, the registers do not indicate any sharp fall under Edward, nor, unless in divinity, any special decline from Edward to Mary. Here one might pause to wonder about the sources of this fairly steady flow of university students, a flow which markedly increased from the beginning of Elizabeth's reign. Was the destruction of schools, even under Edward, so wholesale as many early and recent commentators have made out?

Contemporary witnesses, like modern ones, contradicted

one another, and some, like Ascham, contradicted themselves. Men's vision was strongly colored by religious and political as well as personal prejudice. Further, like academic men in all ages, they were much given to hasty expressions of rhetorical pessimism. There was disagreement not only between Protestants and Catholics but among Protestants as to the nature and causes of the decline in learning; a main theme on both sides was the fear of an inadequate supply of learned clergy. I have used some figures about enrollment because modern historians have so often been content to echo the vague lamentations of contemporaries or of Fuller and Anthony Wood. In that respect the decline seems to have been much exaggerated. The more important and difficult question of a decline in morale we have partly touched, and here too we may think the case somewhat overdrawn, though at best it was serious enough.

In this brief sketch of the educational problem something has been said incidentally in defense of Henry VIII. While I am not trying to whitewash him, but only to remove a few layers of the mud indiscriminately hurled by Mr. Chambers, I should like to add a few words more about Henry's policy and achievement. We have observed his founding or refounding of important schools and colleges. He seriously desired to provide a supply of educated men for the service of state and church, and one piece of evidence is the establishment of scholarships. In 1536 a royal injunction required every priest with emoluments of one hundred pounds or more to maintain a scholar at a university or grammar school. We do not know how effective this rule was, but it may be supposed to have worked pretty well, since it was re-enacted under Edward and again under Elizabeth. One minor but not insignificant advance was the authorization of what was called Lily's *Grammar* as the textbook in all grammar schools.

For further evidence of Henry's support of education and the new learning one may quote the injunctions to Cambridge of 1535. "He inciteth them to the study of tongues. . . . He enjoineth them to found, on the joint cost of all the Colleges, two Lectures, the one of Latin, the other of Greek, to be daily read, (and, by consequence, heard), on great penalties." Duns Scotus and his tribe are banished, along with canon law, and in their place is required the study of Aristotle, Rudolph Agricola, Melanchthon, and others. The "Master of the Sentences" is to give way to the Bible. Mr. Chambers' sniff at Henry's few readerships presumably includes not only the lectureships just mentioned but the Regius Professorships founded at Cambridge and Oxford, which from the first had some distinguished incumbents and greatly stimulated learning in Greek, Hebrew, civil law, medicine, and theology. In regard to all these reforms it may be said that Henry himself was not bearing the cost, or that the ideas were not original with him. To frame an answer on the lowest possible level, one may say first, according to an ancient proverb, that a thief gives all he does not take, and, secondly, on the same principle, that a ruler deserves credit for all the acts he does not veto.

Let us recall the Phillimore-Chambers theory of the effect of More's execution: "In England, all learning felt the blow, and shrank. It was not till the days of Bentley that classical scholarship recovered in England the position it held in the days of Erasmus, before Henry axed it." Erasmus' teaching of Greek at Cambridge in 1511–1514 may have given a great impetus to the English Reformation, but in the matter of Greek scholarship it was a sad disillusionment for the teacher. Greek did not really begin at Cambridge until 1518, when Richard Croke was brought, under Henry's auspices, from an illustrious professorship at Leipzig. Henry was not responsible for the prolonged hostility to Greek which broke out in the "Trojan" war at Oxford in the same year. Nor did Henry dictate Gardiner's fierce and repeated decrees against the reformed pronunciation of Greek inaugurated by Smith and Cheke, decrees which, said Ascham in his impetuous way, almost extinguished all zeal for learning in Cambridge. In these things, and in others which must be passed by, we have, not at all the effect of More's execution, but the bitter antagonism of Catholic adherents of the old learning, whose attitude toward Greek and humanism was generally very different from More's. The reactionaries would have kept the universities tied to degenerate scholasticism if it had not been for a few powerful supporters of humanism, and, though full honor is due to such men as Fisher and Fox, the dominant factor was that Henry was on the side of the new learning.

We might name an unbroken succession of eminent classical scholars throughout the long blank period that Mr. Chambers deplores, but we can glance at only the beginning of it, say the dozen years following the death of More, when the paralysis of humanism might be supposed to be at its worst. And as soon as we look at those years, we realize that we are considering the one period in English history before Bentley when classical studies in an English university were a matter of international fame, when Sir John Cheke taught Cambridge and King Edward Greek. At Cambridge, in this period of arrested humanism, we have, in addition to Cheke and Sir Thomas Smith, both Regius Professors, Ascham himself, William Grindall, William Cecil, Thomas Watson, James Pilkington, and William Bill. Of these men all but Smith were at St. John's. Among other notable scholars in the two universities were Walter Haddon, John Ponet, John Redman, Robert Pember, John Caius, Thomas Wilson, Nicholas Carr, Nicholas Ridley, John Aylmer, Matthew Parker. Nearly all these men were Protestants. Catholics were not paralyzed by the death of More; they were in general, as I said, exponents of the old learning, even when, as in some cases, they were not unfriendly to the new. Here we might recall that young friend of More, Thomas Lupset, who would have been an ornament of this age if he had not died in early manhood. And, though he was not an academic man, one should name Sir Thomas Elyot, one of the most authentic humanists of the century. Of these names many, of course, mean little now except to scholars, but in their day — or should one say in their night? — they were bright beacons, and a respectable number of them are important still. Among the successors of Colet and More one could not ask for better exemplars of Christian humanism than Cheke and Ascham. That the later pair are of smaller stature Phillimore and Chambers would perhaps explain by saying (after *1066 and All That*) that they were not angels but Anglicans.

One general point urged by Phillimore, and at least implied by Mr. Chambers, seems to me fundamental. No Tudor classical scholar, says Phillimore, can be compared for a moment with Lambin and Turnèbe; classical scholarship in England, say both men, did not recover itself until the days of Bentley. In other words, the failure in England to produce any great works of pure scholarship is a mark of arrested development. So far as the humanists were drawn into ecclesiastical controversy, we may regret the conditions which fostered much vain writing and speaking, but otherwise the notion of arrested development betrays a misunderstanding of the vital spirit of English humanism. Of course a number of the humanists wrote little or nothing because, like the fifteenth-century humanists before them, they were busy academic and ecclesiastical administrators — or perhaps they seemed busier than they were. Moreover, the mere burden of teaching borne by such men as Cheke was far greater than that of modern professors. But the real truth lies much deeper than these external circumstances, and it is strange that Phillimore and Mr. Chambers, in contemplating their idol, should not have been saved from an obvious fallacy. More did not seek to rival Scaliger, nor did Erasmus envy the reputation of Budé. Erasmus and More did not investigate the coinage or the grammar of the ancients; they sought to make the rational wisdom of antiquity supplement the teaching of Christ. "You," wrote Erasmus to Budé, "have preferred to be understood by the learned, I, if I can, by the many; your aim is to conquer, mine to teach or persuade." The main impulse of Tudor humanism, and of the best Continental humanism, was not that life should be given up to classical learning, but that classical learning should be an aid to the active Christian life. *The Praise of Folly* and *Utopia*, *The Governour* and *The Schoolmaster*, remain living books. Who except the scholar has heard of Lambin and Turnèbe, and how many scholars could say fifty words about either? I am not disparaging the work of these and other men who did so much to enlarge and purify classical learning, but we should never forget that the purpose of Tudor humanism was education. The broad aim was training in virtue and good letters, the special aim was preparing young men for public life. It was these Tudor humanists who established what was to remain the ruling motive of English classical study down to the days of "the Jowett mind." Would it have been better that William Cecil should continue as a classical don, and perhaps crown his life with an edition of Aristotle's *Politics*, than that he should apply ancient wisdom to practical statesmanship — not without help from Machiavelli? Classical scholars, pure and simple, have always been rare accidents in England. For scholarship means discovery, humanism means discipline. A. E. Housman (like Bentley) believed that the function of a classical scholar in these times was the emending of texts, preferably those of bad poets. Erasmus and More, and Cheke and Ascham and Smith, would have given their approval to Sir Alfred Zimmern and Professor Gilbert Murray for working at Geneva.

So, instead of talking of the blank in classical scholarship down to the days of Bentley, I should say that the appearance of Bentley marked the death of classical humanism. When literature ceases to be studied as a guide to life, the zest for discovery begins. The modern world has long abandoned the didactic and religious view of literature which the best Renaissance humanists held, in common with most of the ancients, and far more has been lost than has been gained in the process. The chief loss was to humanism itself. Renaissance humanism did not rise, as is commonly said, in opposition to theology and religion; it rose mainly in opposition to irreligious and "unhuman" science and philosophy. It strove, as so many movements have striven, to reassert human values, which meant also divine values, against barren logic or a philosophy of nature which neglected the truly human and divine. When the life finally went out of Christian humanism, when the study of literature and rhetoric was divorced from the pursuit of virtue, science regained the ascendancy it had held in the thirteenth and fourteenth centuries. To hungry sheep who felt that they were being fed on husks, the scientists seemed to offer something real. Contemplating a good deal of modern literary scholarship, including one's own minute share in it (but not including Mr. Chambers' robust work), one might be tempted to draw a moral for the present. One might even have the quaint thought that if many of us Renaissance scholars had lived during the Renaissance, we would have been unregenerate Scotists, wrapped up in our quiddities. But it is more discreet to stop here. "Saint Socrates, pray for us."

The Humanist Critic

I HAVE a very simple mind, and my simple creed could be set forth in a paragraph. But it is a matter of strong conviction, and, though a degree of emotional fervor is not an adequate substitute for the intellectual subtlety of modern criticism, I can at least claim to represent the body of common readers in all ages. While my articles of faith are few and elementary, it will take a little space to explain why they are what they are and why I feel strongly about them; and I should like to provide some perspective with a brief sketch of recent developments in scholarship and criticism, however familiar these may be.

Various approaches, old and new, from appreciative impressionism to Marxist dogmatism, have shown both their varying utility and their deficiencies and dangers, but I shall look only at the two chief kinds of criticism, which often lock horns nowadays, the historical and the analytical.

If it is self-evident that literary works produced in our day are conditioned by the impact of our whole civilization upon the writer, it is no less self-evident that that holds for every writer and work of the past. Logically and ideally, therefore, historical criticism is committed to the knowledge and application of all branches of cultural history. Actually, of course, the historical critic does what he can with those segments of knowledge that he is able to com-

Originally published as the sixth in a series of credos in *The Kenyon Review*, Winter 1951; reprinted by permission.

pass. Like the coral animals of bygone theory, he adds his mite to the sum total of historical learning and criticism and expires, having helped, some would say, to build such a coral reef of background and bibliography that no one can get at the work of art itself. Yet the thoroughly justifiable aim is so to re-create all aspects of the past that we can make ourselves virtual contemporaries of an author and understand his intention and achievement in the light of his own age. The method may be most completely successful for those authors who most simply reflect their age, but it is no less essential for those who transcend it. It is only through historical scrutiny that we can distinguish, in both ideas and technique, between the commonplace and the original, between historical and permanent significance. If we see more in a work than its own age saw, or perhaps more than its author saw, historical criticism keeps reinterpretation within bounds; and the historical critic would say that there are such bounds — even if historical interpreters themselves sometimes go off the rails.

Some typical aims and achievements of historical criticism might be illustrated by a couple of examples, and first by a glance at Shakespeare. Whatever the penetrating insights of Lamb, Hazlitt, Keats, and above all Coleridge, romantic criticism was unhistorical and undramatic. Although the final elaboration of the nineteenth-century attitude, Bradley's *Shakespearean Tragedy*, remains an experience for students, modern criticism has taken a very different line. Historical scholarship re-created the conditions under which Shakespeare worked, and saw him, not as a poet writing dramatic poems to be studied in private, but as a man of the theatre appealing with dramatic immediacy to an Elizabethan audience. This emphasis on the plays as dramas has been developed especially by Professor Stoll, who has combined historical scholarship with wide-ranging aesthetic criticism. It is possible of course to carry the theatrical point of view too far, to slight the total patterns and particular subtleties of image and symbol that may seem to belong more to poetry than to the Elizabethan stage, and some recent critics have revived or reinterpreted Shakespeare the poet as against Shakespeare the practical playwright. This new romanticism has its obvious pitfalls too.

The generations of American scholars just before our own were for the most part concerned with literary sources and influences, especially in medieval literature. The finest and one of the last monuments of this kind of scholarship, *The Road to Xanadu*, was not of course medieval, and Professor Lowes's imaginative reconstruction was far above the common process of bricklaying. But even on the lower levels this kind of scholarship accomplished a great deal; the seven seas of literature were charted with a learned thoroughness that must inspire respect, if not excitement, and that at least prepared the way for informed criticism.

Purely literary and historical research, however, could be external and mechanical, and many of the younger generation desired objects and methods more fully in keeping with the high significance of literature in their own lives. One result was a new concern with the history of ideas; another was "the new criticism." To speak of the former, it would be hard to name any period that has not been illuminated by exploration of religious, philosophical, scientific, and other branches of thought; and most of the major writers, poets especially, have been reinterpreted in the new light. For instance, Spenser, Shakespeare, Donne, and Milton, indeed about all the authors of the sixteenth and seventeenth centuries, have been studied in relation to the whole pattern of beliefs and ideas that goes under the name of Christian humanism. The cultivation of other areas has yielded similarly rich fruit. But while the history of ideas has enlightened us in all directions, it has its liabilities. The most obvious one is a tendency to lose the work of art in its philosophical background, to isolate its ideas and treat it as a document, a process in which great works may be reduced to the level of poor ones. The method in itself carries no standard of values — though its exponents may.

In opposition to, or as supplementary to, both literary and philosophical history arose the "new" analytical or aesthetic criticism (which began with the Greeks). This method, inaugurated by men of letters rather than professional scholars, has attracted so many of the younger academic intelligentsia that most departments of English are divided between the "Auld Lichts" and the "New Lichts." While the new critics differ among themselves, they are united by some common principles. Their aim also is to re-create and share the author's original experience, although, it generally appears, within the limits of language and technique rather than in its totality. But if the end of all scholarship and criticism is the elucidation of works of art, the new criticism may be said to come nearest to that end. It has done and is doing great service in teaching a slack-minded generation how to read, and in replacing vague impressionism with rigorous, concrete analysis. Like other methods, however, this one may seem to have its liabilities. One is a practical if not theoretical indifference to the historical method that may result in incomplete or misleading interpretations. Another seems to be a definition of poetry that virtually excludes everything that is not in the "metaphysical" tradition. Finally, it seems to me that this method cannot be said, any more than other methods, to be based on any satisfying criteria of value (apart from technical values). Critics conditioned by modern scientific skepticism, who maintain a detached scientific objectivity, seem to assume that literature is written and read with the aesthetic intelligence only, and to hold aloof from the elementary but central things that have always made literature a necessity of life. These objections may be ill-founded, but they can arise in the mind of an outsider who is not, especially in regard to the last point, prepared to take so much for granted.

The historical and analytical methods that have been touched upon, and other methods, such as the psychological, that have not been touched, have their evident merits and shortcomings, and one moral that emerges from the briefest discussion is that no one approach is adequate by itself. It may be hoped that all students of literature endorse, in theory at least, all scholarly and critical means and methods that contribute to understanding, from technical bibliography to aesthetic contemplation. Obviously talents do not come in a plenary shower, and most of us can only row a skiff, not an eight-oared shell. But it is important, for the harmonious well-being of literary studies, that all students, whatever line they themselves follow, should recognize the value of other methods and not condemn them out of hand as wrong-headed and futile. In connection with the whole subject it might be observed that criticism has of late years been elevated from the essential but humble role of acolyte to priestly sanctity and authority, and it is always well to remember that most of the greatest writings we have were composed in periods when scholarship and criticism were either unborn or unweaned.

However, scholarship and criticism are no doubt here to stay, and the problem is the range and direction of such activity. The methods we have noticed, essential as they are, do not, it may be thought, furnish an answer to the ultimate question — why we should read literature at all. It is obviously a good thing to know the literature and culture of the past, but historical knowledge is not an end in itself. It is obviously a good thing that our aesthetic sensibilities or nervous systems should be stimulated, but that also is not an adequate end in itself. What is the ultimate end, according to my creed, is that literature is ethical, that it makes us better. It is hardly necessary to say that I do not take literature to be a branch of homiletics. And I do not mean what many educationists seem to believe, that it is a decorative appendage to civics. That notion is only a deformed and flat-footed ghost of what I do mean, the creed that was central in Greek and Roman antiquity, in the Middle Ages, in the Renaissance, and well up into the nineteenth century. To mention the men who have held this creed would be to catalogue most of the great names in literature, and not merely critics but imaginative writers. In the course of its long reign this creed operated in various ways, on various levels of sophistication, but in essence it was unchanged; and many great writers, from Aristophanes to Milton, from Pope to Tolstoy, were avowedly didactic. Unless literature is in its effect didactic (I repeat the unpleasant word), I do not know any sufficient reason for its existence, at least on the higher planes that we are here concerned with. That is not to say that all ethical writers have been conscious teachers, or that even conscious teachers have not had other and perhaps stronger motives, or that readers go to literature as they go to the doctor or the psychiatrist.

That throughout its golden ages literature has been conceived of as didactic, and that many of the greatest writers have regarded their office as priestlike, is not a naive theory but a plain historical fact, though it is stated here with unqualified brevity. If most great literature from Homer and the Bible to, say, Conrad (to name only one especially positive modern moralist) has fortified and enriched the human spirit, why should the guardians and expositors of literature so largely remain outside the inner shrine of ethical-aesthetic experience? While it is a main part of the critic's function to display the imaginative and artistic power of literature, it is surely no less essential that he be a moralist, that he try to appraise its ethical value. It is no objection that critical moralists, from Plato to Irving Babbitt, could have their excesses and shortcomings; so do critics and scholars who pursue other interests. Most of the great critics of the past have been more or less ethical in their judgments, and the need of such criticism was never greater than it is now, when the confusion and loss of ethical values is the most familiar and paralyzing of clichés, and when philosophy has abandoned its traditional ethical concerns in order to become the tail to the scientific kite. Even on the most general grounds it might seem that what was fundamental throughout the great past would be our best guide for the present and future. Without slighting either historical knowledge or aesthetic analysis, I should like to see the study of literature fired by something like the spirit with which George Chapman approached Homer's Achilles and Odysseus (if I may use again a favorite quotation):

> In one, predominant perturbation; in the other, overruling wisdom: in one, the body's fervour and fashion of outward fortitude to all possible height of heroical action; in the other, the mind's inward, constant, and unconquered empire; unbroken, unaltered, with any most insolent and tyrannous infliction.

If the modern mind is confused about ethical values, it is still more so about religion — unless it rests securely in a simple naturalism that begs all the questions; and the recent symposium, "Religion and the Intellectuals," suggests that a number of the finer minds are not less befuddled than the rest of us. I have assuredly no revelation to offer. But I do think that we can achieve a partial conquest of disorder by submitting ourselves to the literature of the sixteenth and seventeenth centuries. The classical-Christian beliefs and ideas that made up the general creed of that age may be no longer tenable in themselves, but the great and less great writers who held them possessed an ethical and religious vision of man and life that is, one may think, more comprehensive, more central, more realistic, more satisfying, than is commonly found in the great writers of later times. And a bath in that literature has a restorative power. Against its ethical sanity and religious insight, its double vision of man as both a god and a beast, may be measured those later writers who, with the decline of the old religious and ethical tradition, became more subject to individual confusions and aberrations. If the modern mind is to find the "truth," it seems to me that we are more likely to find it through the past than in a present and future increasingly cut off from the past. The process of severance, which may be said to have been begun by Descartes, is being completed by modern positivism. Since the positivist brushes aside religion and metaphysics as meaningless, he can hardly help brushing aside traditional intuitive ethics also. If the literature of the past which is ethical and religious and metaphysical is to be thrown out, and the writer of the future is to live on the husks of a "scientific morality," we are indeed entering a new Dark Age. The loss of an active consciousness of our religious, ethical, and cultural tradition is a much worse menace than atomic or hydrogen bombs; and if critics do not labor to preserve and fructify it, who will?

Another article of my creed has been implied already, that one function of criticism is to reach people outside the inner circle of initiates, to make untrue the painful saying that a liberal education ends on Commencement Day, to "make reason and the will of God prevail." (One encounters sniffs at Arnold's lack of analytical power, or his lack of historical knowledge, but he was in the great tradition of criticism.) I do not think that this or that exclusive end can be set up as a permanent absolute; needs vary from age to age. We needed more historical knowledge and more technical analysis, and both instruments will continue to be needed. But it seems to me that at the present time, when culture is threatened by barbarism within as well as without, the most urgent function of criticism is not to enlarge the learning of the learned, or to refine the perceptions of the refined, but to enlarge and refine the saving remnant. If this be damned as propagandist heresy, so be it.

As a matter of fact, I am only wishing for a fuller return to the broad and central road of criticism. If we look at the last few decades and then at the many earlier centuries, we must conclude that most of our problems are of recent origin, that it is the modern approach to literature that has become divided and complicated — a situation that is very unhappy at a time when the voice of scientists and social scientists, a voice that is not still nor small, proclaims that they have blueprints and statistics for saving a muddled world. Some symptoms have grown so familiar that we take them as normal: that the body of general readers, who were once the mainstay of literature, has dwindled into groups of self-conscious highbrows; that people genuinely interested in the literature of the past are an infinitesimal fraction of the reading public, and that few college graduates, even among those who majored in literature, read much beyond the contemporary or the ephemeral after leaving college; that scholarship and criticism have become the small preserve of academic specialists who write mainly for one another. While it may be granted that cultural disintegration is not a new phenomenon of our age, it is also notorious that it has of late been especially rapid and radical.

A glance beyond our age, however, indicates that, from the time of Sir Philip Sidney up through the nineteenth century, critics wrote mainly for the general body of cultivated readers, readers whose knowledge, taste, and outlook were much the same as the writers.' There was one language, that of educated people; there was not our variety of jargons developed by various professional tribes and now partly taken over into criticism. Both writers and readers had as a rule a substantial and uniform education. There was a cultural tradition that commanded general allegiance and sustained established values. That this relatively unified and conservative tradition had its drawbacks one would not of course deny, but, looking back upon it in 1950, one may feel some envy. Moreover, such conservative solidarity did not prevent the emergence of a higher proportion of writers of genius than our enormously enlarged English-speaking world can now show.

It seems to me that we have paid much too high a price for the rapid advancement of knowledge, not merely in science but in literature as well. The extreme specialization that has made such advancement possible has impoverished us as individuals and helped to disintegrate the cultural tradition, to isolate literary students from one another and from the public. Neither scholars nor critics have given much attention to the common reader. If the common reader is now almost extinct, or devotes his time to books on Russia and atomic energy, or has delivered her soul to the book clubs, the process of reconversion will be uphill work.

Most of the active forces in our civilization are against us — as they always have been against the humanities, even in more auspicious times. Moreover, if the scholar or critic does address the public (in anything except a biography), his efforts will be largely ignored by lowbrow, middlebrow, and highbrow reviews alike. None the less, I think the effort ought to be continually made. Unless modern man is hopelessly debilitated and corrupted, we must believe that he cannot live without the humanities, and that he will in time respond if scholars and critics keep the humanities alive and humane. We scholars might have in mind the fate of the ancient classics and ask ourselves if our historical projects are or ought to be of interest to even a theoretical *homo sapiens*. And the critics might ask themselves if their exegesis is or ought to be of interest to even a superior type of *homo sapiens*. And members of both parties might ask themselves if their enterprises would have the blessing, say, of Chaucer, Shakespeare, and Milton, who were not merely gentlemen of letters. I do not mean that there ought to be a law against esoteric inquiries; I only mean that the main energies of literary study should aim at a common denominator. We may remember that Sidney, Ben Jonson, Dryden, Addison, Pope, Dr. Johnson, Coleridge, Arnold, and others did not address academic scholars or academic critics but the whole body of cultivated readers. If there is now no such body, then it needs to be created by critical and pedagogical exertion.

To mention these critics is to be reminded that they — and their Continental counterparts — were all brought up on the classics, that they belonged to an unbroken tradition; and we might allow ourselves to be startled by the paradoxical fact that, while the great bulk of English and other modern literatures is closely related to Latin and Greek, an increasing majority of professional students do not read either language. (Our academic forebears, who generally knew both, were intent only upon preserving a knowledge of Gothic.) We might, as Professor Ernest Hunter Wright suggested a while ago, require Latin and Greek for the Ph.D., though the imagination falters at the reconstruction of our whole educational system that that would entail. Yet every teacher may wonder how long the great writing of the past can be understood and appreciated by readers ignorant even of Latin, and what the non-Latinist makes of the great effects of Anglo-Saxon and classical combinations in English prose and poetry — not to mention the body of classical literature, which zealous students can read "in translation." But if our "creed" is to deal only with things possible, I will not list belief in a classical education as a tenet; this is only a nostalgic footnote — and a declaration that I do not think the value of the classics has been outmoded by psychology and anthropology.

To sum up these far from novel or fashionable observations, I believe that criticism should use all helpful means and methods for the study of literature; that historical knowledge and aesthetic analysis need to work together, and preferably in the same mind, not in different minds; that, our outer and inner worlds being what they now are, the scholar or critic cannot be content with the elucidation of works of art, central as that function is; that he has the further and traditional function of actively conserving the ethical and cultural inheritance that we are in danger of losing altogether; and that he has a social or (if the word be allowed) a missionary obligation, to labor to convert the heathen. If my position is naive, reactionary, and unrealistic, I can only say that I would rather go to hell with a Christian Platonist than to heaven with a naturalistic positivist.

The Humanities

No one would ever speak of "the plight of the natural sciences," or of "the plight of the social sciences," but it is always proper to speak of "the plight of the humanities," and in the hushed, melancholy tone of one present at a perpetual deathbed. For something like twenty-five hundred years the humanities have been in more or less of a plight, not because they are themselves weak, but because their war is not merely with ignorance but with original sin; and as civilization has advanced, the means of stultifying the head and heart have multiplied in variety and power. As a sample of cultural leadership, or of a common attitude, I should like to read a declaration of faith delivered some years ago by the chairman of the department of humanities in a well-known technological institution. We will call him Professor X. This is most of the report, from the *New York Times*, of his speech to a convention of engineers:

> Professor X . . . asserted last night that it would be "morally wrong" for him to advise the reading of the literary classics in this fast-moving age of television, radio and movies. . . .
>
> One should read for the purpose of doing something with what one reads, he asserted: not of polishing one's mind like a jewel, but of improving the world around.
>
> Take up a book because it will tell you something of the world

This address, delivered on October 14, 1954, in Chicago at the 37th annual meeting of the American Council on Education, is reprinted by permission from the January 1955 issue of *The Educational Record*. Part of it appeared in *The New York Times Magazine*, January 9, 1955, and it was subsequently printed in *The Key Reporter*, Spring 1955.

. . . ; read what you want to read, not what you think you should read. "This is the frame of mind that makes reading worthwhile and often deeply rewarding.

"For example, it would be morally wrong of me to urge you to take up a classic like 'David Copperfield' and to settle yourselves in easy chairs for winter evenings' reading. If you tried 'David Copperfield' you would grow restive; you would think of all the other things you might be doing more consistent with your daily environment — looking at television, listening to the radio, going to the movies.

"Moreover, you would wonder why you should spend so much time laboriously reading 'David Copperfield' when you could see the book as a film, should it return some time to the neighborhood movie." . . . .

"The single prescription for adult reading," he added, "should be to read something different, something that will change your mind. Herein lies compensation for the loss of the purely reflective life."

Engineers are not, to be sure, in common repute the most cultivated branch of mankind, but did even they deserve such counsel, and from such a source? The humanities, as I said, have always had to contend with the crude urges of the natural man, with his resistance to higher values than his own, but the speech I just quoted from reminds us of the many new ways there are of escaping from active thought and feeling into a state of lazy collapse, of passive surrender to unthinking action or external sensation. Many people would endorse our oracle's view that one should not read to polish one's mind like a jewel but for the sake of improving the world around. The humanistic tradition has always stood for improvement of the world, but it has always insisted that a man must make himself worthy of such an enterprise; one of our perennial troubles is that improvement of the world is undertaken by so many unpolished minds. Then our touching faith in machinery is illustrated by the quaint assumption that a movie is the same thing as a great book. And that Ersatz doctrine extends down through television to the comics, which have now joined the march of mind by reducing literary classics to capsule form. That sort of thing, by the way, was done, and done much better, a dozen centuries ago, and has been commonly labeled a symptom of the Dark Ages. But this is only a reminder; there is no need of enlarging upon such powerful elements in our popular civilization. The opposition to such elements comes from the humanities.

Negative terms, however, are not enough. The "humanities," in the original meaning of this and kindred words, embraced chiefly history, philosophy, and literature. These were the studies worthy of a free man, that ministered to *homo sapiens*, man the intellectual and moral being, and not to *homo faber*, the professional and technical expert. And these, with divinity, completed the central circle of human knowledge and understanding. Divinity went overboard long ago; history, which once was literature, is now a social science; and philosophy, though still grouped with the humanities, has become a branch of mathematics. Thus in common usage the humanities mean literature and the fine arts. That is an unfortunate narrowing but we may take things as we find them and concentrate on literature, which is central and representative.

One plain fact nowadays is that the study of literature, which in itself is comprehensive and complex, has had to take over the responsibilities that used to be discharged by philosophy and divinity. Most young people now get their only or their chief understanding of man's moral and religious quest through literature. Anyone who has been teaching literature for twenty-five or thirty years, as I have, can testify to the marked change there has been in the spiritual climate during that time. (A rigorously scientific colleague of mine, in psychology, will not permit the use of the word "spiritual," but I use it anyhow.) I am speaking mainly of the higher order of college students, but it would be hard to imagine even the better students of twenty-five or thirty years ago reading Dante and George Herbert and Milton and Hopkins and Eliot with the real sympathy that many now show. For the more intelligent and sensitive young people of today, and there are very many of that kind, are a serious and a conservative lot. They not only live in our unlovely world, they have no personal experience of any other. They are aware of hollowness and confusion all around them, and, what is still more real, of hollowness and confusion in themselves. They feel adrift in a cockboat on an uncharted sea, and they want a sense of direction, of order and integration. And in literature they find, as countless people have found before them, that their problems are not new, that earlier generations have been lost also. Most of the young people I see find in literature, literature of the remote past as well as of the present, what they cannot find in textbooks of psychology and sociology, the vision of human experience achieved by a great spirit and bodied forth by a great artist.

I apologize for elaborating what may be called clichés, but those familiar lists of courses in catalogues make one forget that the frigid label "English 10" or "French 20" may represent an illumination and a rebirth for John or Betty Smith. Not that courses are the only or even the main road to enriched experience and sensitivity, but they are one road; and a teacher can help as a guide or catalyst. Josiah Royce is said to have complained that a philosopher was expected to spiritualize the community. The modern philosopher is expected only to semanticize the community;

the other function, as I said, falls upon the teacher of literature. I do not of course mean inspirational gush. I mean that teachers, conducting a critical discussion of a piece of great literature, necessarily deal not only with the artistic use of words and materials but with the moral and spiritual experience that are its subject matter. That is why, as President Pusey has said, the humanities must be the cornerstone of a liberal education. Naturally teachers will have their methods under constant scrutiny, but their material, the world's great literature, can hardly be improved; all it needs is a chance to work upon responsive minds and characters.

While I cannot guess the temper of this gathering, and while all the administrators present may, for all I know, regard the humanities as a pearl of great price, that is not their general reputation. Administrators are commonly said to prize the solid and tangible virtues of the natural and social sciences and to look upon the humanities as a nice luxury for the carriage trade. How far that general reputation is true or false I wouldn't know, but, just in case it has a modicum of truth, I have been insisting that the humanities are not a luxury; they are the most practical of necessities if men and women are to become fully human. The humanities commonly suffer in esteem because they do not lend themselves to statistical reports of achievement. You cannot demonstrate with graphs and charts that John or Betty Smith, through reacting to a piece of literature, became a person of richer moral and imaginative insight, of finer wisdom and discrimination and stability. For the experience of literature is an individual experience, and nothing that is really important can be measured.

When we look at the American educational scene, the diversity of standards is so great that generalizations about this or that part of it may be violently contradictory. At any rate educational history of the past fifty years seems to furnish a pretty good forecast of the bad effects of the deluge to be expected in the next fifteen. In school, college, and university, the results of the huge increase in the student body suggest that the principle of education for all, however fine in theory, in practice leads ultimately to education for none. An editorial in the *New York Times* of September 13, 1954, takes the usual line of defense. The principle of education for all, it says, forces us "to accept the principle, also, that the function of education is primarily social and political rather than purely intellectual." "It cannot be denied," the *Times* proceeds, "that this means a down-grading of the learning process. We are adjusting to an 'average' that must be spread so widely that it comes down automatically. Education is no longer the intellectual privilege of the gifted few. It is held to be the democratic right of all." The *Times* does go a little beyond this orthodox assent to express uneasiness over the sacrifice, in elementary and secondary schools, of quality to quantity.

To mention one of many results, there has been an appalling growth of illiteracy at all levels, even in the graduate school. (Somehow stenographers are still literate, even if their college-bred employers are not.) At every orgy of Commencements one wonders how many of the hordes of new bachelors of arts can speak and write their own language with elementary decency, or read it with understanding. After all, the polished mind is suspect, whether in a student, a professor, or a Presidential candidate. And illiteracy, and contentment with illiteracy, are only symptoms of general shoddiness.

Obviously one main cause of this state of things has been the sheer pressure of numbers, along with a deplorable shrinkage in the number of qualified teachers. But the situation would not be so bad as it has been if the downward pressure of numbers had not been powerfully strengthened by misguided doctrine and practice. The training of teachers and the control of school curricula have been in the hands of colleges of education and their products, and these have operated on principles extracted from John Dewey's philosophy of barbarism. (If that phrase seems unduly harsh, I may say that I have in mind Dewey's hostility to what he regarded as leisure-class studies; his antihistorical attitude, his desire — intensified in his followers — to immerse students in the contemporary and immediate; and his denial of a hierarchy of studies, his doctrine that all kinds of experience are equally or uniquely valuable; and it would not be irrelevant to add his notoriously inept writing.) The lowest common denominator has been, not an evil, but an ideal. The substantial disciplines have been so denuded of content that multitudes of students, often taught by uneducated teachers, have been illiterate, uninformed, and thoroughly immature. There is no use in priding ourselves on the operation of the democratic principle if education loses much of its meaning in the process. When we think, for instance, of education for citizenship, which has been the cry of modern pedagogy, we may think also of the volume and violence of popular support given to the anti-intellectual demagoguery of the last few years. Mass education tends to reflect mass civilization, instead of opposing it. Even if education were everywhere working on the highest level, it would still face tremendous odds.

The great problem has been, and will be, first, the preservation of minority culture against the many and insidious pressures of mass civilization, and, secondly, the extension of that minority culture through wider and wider areas.

The rising flood of students is very much like the barbarian invasions of the early Middle Ages, and then the process of education took a thousand years. We hope for something less overwhelming, and for a less protracted cure, but the principle is the same; Greco-Roman-Christian culture not only survived but triumphed, and with enrichment. If we think of our problem in the light of that one, we shall not be disheartened but recognize both as phases of man's perennial growing pains.

Throughout history it has been a more or less small minority that has created and preserved what culture and enlightenment we have, and, if adverse forces are always growing, that minority is always growing too. In spite of the low standards that have commonly prevailed in public education during the last fifty years, I think the top layer of college students now are proportionately more numerous than they were thirty years ago and are more generally serious and critical. There is a growing nucleus of fine minds, and teachers are concerned with the enlargement of that all-important group. At the same time, without retreating from that position, one wonders what it is in our educational process or in our culture at large that often causes a liberal education to end on Commencement Day.

I have no novel and dramatic remedy for the evils that have shown themselves so clearly already and will become more formidable still. But I might mention a few things of varying importance which do not seem utopian. Of course I represent no one but myself, and I cannot even say, like a member of the House of Lords, that I enjoy the full confidence of my constituents.

In the first place, I see no reason why the flood of students should be allowed to pour into college, why automatic graduation from school should qualify anyone for admission. We ought to recognize, and make people in general recognize, that a desire for economic or social advantage, or for merely four years of idle diversion, is not enough. Under such pressure as is coming, surely the state universities have the strength to set up bars and select their student body, instead of admitting all who choose to walk in the front door and then, with much trouble and expense, trying to get rid of some through the back door. Doubtless such procedure would require a campaign of enlightenment and persuasion, but legislators always have an alert ear for the cry of economy, and the public must be convinced that higher education, or what passes for that, is neither a birthright nor a badge of respectability, and that useful and happy lives can be led without a college degree. As things are, we have an army of misfits, who lower educational standards and increase expense, and no branch of a university staff has grown more rapidly of late years than the psychiatric squad.

Secondly, many people have grounds for the belief that the multiplying junior colleges can and will drain off a large number of the young who for various reasons are unfitted for a really strenuous four-year course. Junior colleges, however, should not be recreational centers for the subnormal.

Thirdly, I think the need for formal education beyond high school would be much lessened, and the quality of both secondary and higher education obviously improved, if the colleges and universities, getting the public behind them, make a concerted and effectual demand that the schools do their proper work and do it much better than a great many schools have been doing it.[1] Quite commonly,

[1] Since 1955 there seems to have been a good deal of improvement, though the ideal is still some way ahead.

a distressing proportion of a college course now consists of high-school work. For instance, we have grown so accustomed to a battalion of instructors teaching elementary composition to freshmen that we take it as a normal part of college education, whereas in fact it is a monstrosity. Imagine a European university teaching the rudiments of expression! If high-school graduates are illiterate, they have no business in college. For a long time, and for a variety of reasons, we have had slackness all along the line; somehow, sometime, strictness and discipline have got to begin.

Increased enrollments have almost inevitably led to increased reliance upon large lecture courses. There are administrators who assume that there is no limit to the effectiveness of a lecture course except the size of the auditorium, and there are also some teachers who see positive virtues in lectures and can themselves display them. Perhaps because I never remember anything I hear, I do not share that faith. I favor classes small enough to allow discussion, and they are expensive. But there are possible economies that would be highly desirable in themselves. We do not need to maintain the naive doctrine that there has to be a course in everything or anything in which anyone has ever been or might be interested, and that no one can look into a subject for himself. Further, a good many catalogues list courses that can only be called fantastic, and I do not think I am guilty of partisan prejudice if I say that these are rarely found among the humanities. At any rate, if we had fewer and less specialized courses, and if we did not have our armies of composition teachers, a considerable number of man-hours would be released for smaller classes.

One thing that has suffered grievously and conspicuously in this last generation has been the study of foreign languages. The usual reason given is again the pressure of numbers, the numbers who are not going beyond high school, but again a positive reason has been open or quiet hostility. Languages have been pretty well crowded out of the school curriculum, and of course there has been a corresponding decline in college study. Nothing has been commoner in recent decades than the applicant for admission to a graduate school who has had little or no acquaintance with any foreign language except possibly a year or two of Spanish. Serious study of a foreign language means work, and a first principle of modern pedagogy has been the elimination of work. Thus, during the years in which we have all become conscious of one small world, and in which this country has become the leader of that world, educational theory and practice have retreated into cultural parochialism. There is no need to argue how necessary for the ordinary citizen is some knowledge of a foreign language and a foreign people. In the last few years a good many parents have been aroused, and the Modern Language Association has been putting on a vigorous campaign, so that progress has been made; but there is a long way to go. It is encouraging that in some cities successful experiments have been made in the teaching of languages in elementary schools, where, for good psychological reasons, they ought to begin. I wish there were something encouraging to be said about the ancient languages, but we are concerned with actualities.

Finally, since I touched on the large number of young people who are in college and should not be, I might mention those who are not and should be, and who may be lost in the oncoming flood. Educators and others are more conscious than they once were of our failure to recognize and foster promising students who cannot afford college, and increasing efforts are being made in that direction; but we are still very far behind England, where bright students are picked out at the age of ten or eleven and brought along on scholarships. If we spent on exceptional students a fraction of the time and money we have spent on nursing lame ducks, there would be a considerable change in the quality of education.

One last word on a different matter. Like everything else, the Ph.D. has been cheapened by quantitative pressure, and it might be earnestly wished that it were not a union card for the teaching profession. There are plenty of young men and women who would be good teachers without such a degree, and the degree itself ought to mean something more than it does. Along with that may go another earnest wish, that both administrators and members of departments would abandon the principle of "Publish or perish." Socrates would never have had a chance at an assistant professorship.

Tradition and Experience

THE PROBLEM of poetry and belief, if not quite so old as poetry itself, is at least as old as philosophy. We remember Plato's account of the efforts of mythographers to explain away, by means of allegory, the indecorous behavior of Homer's gods. The same kind of problem arose early in the Christian era: miracles in both the Old and the New Testament were expounded by some of the church fathers as allegorical, not literal — to the great relief of the young and troubled Augustine. For Christians confronted with pagan literature the well-tried allegorical defense was again invoked, and throughout the Middle Ages allegorical interpretation was carried on. Not only the *Aeneid* but even Ovid's *Metamorphoses* was revamped in moral and religious terms. Such interpretations did not of course preclude aesthetic enjoyment. Then there were general handbooks of mythology composed on the same principle; the most famous of the earlier ones was the product of Boccaccio's sober years. Later and more learned handbooks of this kind were written up into the seventeenth century and were used by such poets as Spenser and Chapman and Jonson, as poets of our time have used *The Golden Bough*. The allegorical interpretation of myth went along with a conscious effort to see this body of fable as a corrupted version of

Reprinted by permission from *Literature and Belief: English Institute Essays, 1957*, ed. M. M. Abrams (New York, 1958), biblical truth; the flood described by Ovid was clearly a pagan story of Noah's flood, and so on.

It might be said that in our time the traditional problem has been reversed. Whereas the Middle Ages and the Renaissance were concerned with making pagan literature not only safe but morally helpful for Christian readers, the problem now is to make Christian literature acceptable to predominantly pagan readers in what it has become fashionable to call the post-Christian era. To put the case in that way is doubtless to exaggerate, and some qualifications will be made as we go on. To make a large one now, the problem of poetry and belief takes in far more than religious creeds. Two great poets of our age exemplify opposite poles: while the middle and later Eliot poses the religious problem with full immediacy, the reading of Yeats does not require belief in his fantastic "system." But Yeats is a special illustration of a larger modern problem: a poet of religious temperament, he had been cut off by science from Christianity and felt obliged to construct an imaginative world of symbols in which he could feel at home. In an age dominated by science and scientific method, some people ask if poetry, which is born of individual intuition, can claim any validity at all. In such an age, when scientific truth is commonly regarded as the only kind of truth, Coleridge's classic phrase, "that willing suspension of disbelief for the moment which constitutes poetic faith," may not seem a very positive validation for poetry. I. A. Richards, certainly a friend of poetry — and one who has lately turned poet himself — perhaps betrayed something of our age's scientific bias when he tried to establish poetry on solid ground by calling it pseudo statement, as distinguished from the statements of science.

However, the problem as a whole is much too complicated for one discussion, at least by me, and I should like to concentrate on one question: how far can the non-Christian reader apprehend and assimilate poetry more or less based on Christian belief, and belief of an older and more fundamentalist kind than that of modern liberal Protestantism? This limited but still large question has been much in the air during the last twenty-five years or so, especially because of Mr. Richards' formulations and Mr. Eliot's remarks on the modern reader's approach to Dante. Since I myself do not breathe easily in the rarefied air of aesthetic theory, I should like to pretend that all this modern discussion does not exist and offer, as it were, a first report from the literary equivalent of the man in the street — or perhaps I should say the man in the classroom.

Before we settle down with particular poets, a few more generalities may be allowed. It may be assumed that Christian readers, Catholic or Protestant, have no serious difficulties with either the writings of Catholics or the literature of traditional Protestantism. In many years of teaching Milton, I cannot recall that Catholic students, including priests and nuns, ever had trouble with *Paradise Lost*; and Sister Miriam Joseph has lately written a monograph on the Catholicity of what people have been so much given to calling the Puritan epic.

Some problems do arise for Christian readers of non-Christian literature, which is a large part of the world's writing in prose and verse. Christians of critical sophistication, who are presumably not very numerous, may study and aesthetically enjoy much that they regard as inadequate or erroneous. For Cardinal Newman the study of literature was a plain necessity for people living in the world, but it was also a matter of regret that the mass of the world's literature is "the Life and Remains of the *natural* man," "the science or history, partly and at best of the natural man, partly of man fallen": "I say, from the nature of the case, if Literature is to be made a study of human nature, you cannot have a Christian literature. It is a contradiction in terms to attempt a sinless Literature of sinful man." One may wonder what Newman would have thought of Graham Greene or Mauriac.

No modern reader is likely to apply more rigorously Christian criteria than Professor Hoxie N. Fairchild, whose fourth volume came out this year, and he has found very little English poetry between 1700 and 1880 that is both Christian and poetry, though his active aesthetic sensibility has not been starved. Mr. Fairchild's definition of a religious person — one admittedly inadequate for a Christian — posits belief in the insufficiency of man and the transcendent objectivity of God. Most of us are likely to accept that definition, even if we tend to use it less strictly than he does; and perhaps we might wish to include under religion, as no doubt Mr. Fairchild would, a concern for righteousness and for love. Mr. Fairchild's latest volume covers that special and conspicuous category of poems, from Tennyson, Browning, Arnold, and others, which grapple directly with the Victorian problem of faith and which most people, whatever their degree of doctrinal or aesthetic approval, would call religious, though Mr. Fairchild would not. He avowedly likes the poetry of real belief or real disbelief and dislikes what he considers the idealistic smudges, emotional and verbal, of those poets who grope in twilight; he prefers *The City of Dreadful Night* to *The Dream of Gerontius* — and *The Dream of Gerontius* to *Merlin and the Gleam.* He has much less sympathy with *In Memoriam* than Mr. Eliot has.

We are left with, or return to, the non-Christian reader's

reactions to literature in the Christian tradition, though some general observations may be made before we come to examples. The term "non-Christian" must cover the aggressive atheist (to use an old-fashioned word), the passive agnostic, and what one takes to be the pretty large body of people who, in Charles Williams' phrase, without being themselves Christians are opposed to those who oppose Christianity. They are people who have profound reverence for the character and teaching of Christ, and profound sympathy with the Christian scale of values and the best Christian tradition, but are unable to accept the supernaturalism of the orthodox creed, however liberally that creed be reinterpreted. It may be guessed that such people form a high proportion of those engaged in the teaching and criticism of literature, and it is chiefly they — we are not concerned with imaginative writers — who may be supposed to feel the pressure of the problem of belief. It appears therefore to be in the literal sense a mainly academic problem. But I must say that I think it is also in the abstract sense a mainly academic problem, that it is not nearly so heavy a burden as a multitude of more tangible ills that afflict mankind. If it far outweighed all others, as theoretically it should, most of us would be in a bad way. No doubt those who wander between two worlds would, as persons, be happier and richer if they held a firm dogmatic faith, but, if they cannot achieve that, they must rub along as best they can. And if one must live, so to speak, on the income from unearned capital, one may prefer the capital of the Christian — and classical — inheritance to the more fluid assets of psychology. As readers and critics of Christian literature, such people may be under a partial handicap; yet the amount of great and positively Christian literature is, relatively, not large, and, moreover, a strongly sympathetic knowledge of the Christian tradition is a potent quickener of attachment and insight. To mention a less individual matter, for literature of the sixteenth and the earlier seventeenth century, including Shakespeare, modern students of all kinds have had an invaluable key, or foundation, in the Christian and classical doctrine of order and degree, which was metaphysical, religious, ethical, social, and political. Finally, these indeterminate Laodiceans may possibly be better qualified than some Christians for the understanding of non-Christian writing.

We are thinking of the literature, mainly the poetry, of the Christian era, from Dante onward. It is plain that some technical and aesthetic elements lie outside the question; we cannot distinguish between a Christian and a non-Christian prosody — it might not be irrelevant here to recall George Brandes' remark about Voltaire's verse, that the man who had little respect for anything in heaven or earth respected the uniform caesura of the Alexandrine. But some central elements of technique do lie within the problematic area; structure and language and image may depend upon Christian beliefs and ideas. For a random and simple and tremendous example, George Herbert's *Virtue* moves from everyday phenomena to the final conflagration of the world, the judgment day, and immortality; but the most stubbornly secular reader can hardly fail there in understanding or even in imaginative and emotional response (though a student did once raise a query about the geological formation of coal). Nor, to take a less simple case, can one imagine a reader of *Lycidas* so invincibly skeptical that he is not carried away by the beatific vision that resolves all Milton's questioning of divine providence and justice. The complexities of *Paradise Lost*, and of Dante, may be postponed.

In this connection, readers of the most diverse belief or unbelief may unite in deploring the increasing ignorance of the Bible. Last May, in my examination in Milton, I asked for a short note on the first and third temptations in *Paradise Regained*, and two students, displaying a knowledge of the Bible on a par with their knowledge of Milton, spoke of Christ's being challenged to jump off a cliff. But, lest I give an unjust impression of Harvard and Radcliffe, I hasten to add that many students are conversant with the Bible and that many respond warmly to Milton. The necessity of knowing the Bible — not to mention Christian iconography and related things — needs no proof, though it will have some illustration as we go along. I do not of course mean to suggest that for students of literature the Bible is only a primitive *Golden Bough*.

On the positive side, one general phenomenon that has a large bearing on our problem is too familiar to need description, that is, the revival of religion, or at least of interest in religion, among intellectuals. In recent decades there has been much more respectful recognition of the Christian view of life and man than conventional liberalism used to permit; and indeed one main cause of the change has been a conviction of the inadequacy or bankruptcy of that liberalism. The numerical strength of writers actually committed to the Christian faith may not be great, but among them are poets and critics and religious thinkers who cannot be brushed off as unintelligent. This movement has distinctly altered the literary climate and made sophisticated readers in general much more receptive to religious writings and ideas. Even the secular critic has added to his vocabulary — partly for the discussion of modern literature — such unwonted words as sin, guilt, redemption, nature, grace. And even if we grant the currency of more religiosity than religion, this is still significant evidence of disquietude, of dissatisfaction with liberal nostrums.

Assuming that many or most students of literature are of

the non-Christian but sympathetic group already described, and that the core of the material is poetry in the Christian tradition, I should like to glance briefly at two sets of examples, first at short religious poems and later at some works of the largest scope. My remarks must be summary, and some personal reactions or guesses may be mistaken — in which case I shall no doubt be promptly informed. We might ask first how we react to the great stream of Christian lyrics that flows from the Middle Ages to the middle of the seventeenth century. Few readers, one imagines, are untouched — if they read them — by the purity and power of medieval poems, from *The Dream of the Rood* to *Quia Amore Langueo*; but what we would call their devotional naiveté may keep them outside our world of experience. To leap up to George Herbert, probably every reader divides his poems into a minor and a major category. Most of those that celebrate things ecclesiastical appeal only or mainly, in Coleridge's phrase, to "an affectionate and dutiful child of the Church," whereas Herbert's usually greater poems are greater because they deal with worldly allurements, rebellious self-will, the desire for discipline and humility and for the renewal of spiritual energy, with conflicts and aspirations and defeats and victories that belong to all human life. In an examination in a course of mine I once asked if barriers of belief stood between the religious metaphysicals and the modern reader, and one particularly memorable answer came from a Jewish student who, remarking on the very different tradition in which he had grown up, argued that no one who wished to live above the natural level could fail to be moved by Herbert.

I do not want to overwork Herbert, but his purely religious poetry has a special value for this discussion; and, to report another item from the same course, it seems to me a fact of interest that last year nearly as many undergraduates chose to write papers on Herbert as on Donne, though all Donne's secular poetry was open to them. (Perhaps I should have some qualms about referring to my course on the metaphysical poets because, after this paper was written, a story in *The New Yorker* made use of the course as a kind of nursery or backdrop for adolescent passions.) As for Donne's religious poems, they have their technical and aesthetic interest, which is considerable but not inexhaustible; yet, with a few exceptions, I do not think that, after the first impact, they wear very well. We — I should no doubt say I — read them less as religious poems than as further revelations of Donne's sensibility and technique. And I would say much the same thing of the *Anniversaries*, which Professor Martz has so admirably analyzed; these poems seem to me for the most part personal and historical documents rather than religious poems that actually speak to us — as, for example, the conclusion of Spenser's *Mutability* speaks to us. Whereas Herbert can enter into and act upon our own being, most of Donne's religious poetry remains an external object of intellectual study. I may be inviting still more violent protest if I venture to link with Donne's *Holy Sonnets* the "terrible sonnets" of Hopkins; here again we feel a powerful and painful shock, but can many of us really get inside them, or can they get inside us? And I will add that *The Windhover*, however exciting as a poem, I can feel only dimly as a religious poem; to me the central image seems not to express but to swallow up the religious theme.

Though I may have completely disqualified myself as a witness, I will proceed. If Donne is in the main too special to speak to our condition, so, in another way, is Crashaw. I cannot recall having been aware of any student of any belief or of none who did not respond to Herbert's "Love bade me welcome." I cannot recall anyone who did respond to *The Weeper* or the more flamboyant odes — a fact that may only reflect upon the expositor. On the other hand, every reader not only possesses Marvell's *Bermudas* with spontaneous ease but understands the subtle delineation of irreligious pride in *The Coronet.* It might be supposed that Vaughan's flashes of vision — quite apart from his poetic lapses — would place him in the category of poets not generally accessible to the modern reader, but I have not found it so, although he does stand somewhat farther from the center than Herbert. If the inference from all these notes and queries is not too obvious to be stated, it is that — various kinds of artistic power being taken for granted — the great poetry of religious meditation, the poetry that really comes home to modern readers who do not share the beliefs it embodies, is that which extends beyond the particular creed and personality of its author, which grows out of and embraces general human experience. And to these seventeenth-century examples might be added, for the same reason, such a rare modern work as *Four Quartets.* Even if a reader views the Christian story and Christian symbols as no more than archetypal myths, his doing so is a recognition of their experiential validity, their truth to life.

To take a wider sweep, we might now look briefly at four or five authors of major works, of whom some wrote about life in general, some almost wholly on religious themes.

One cannot imagine any creed, unless perhaps hard-boiled Marxism, that could interfere with a modern reader's wholehearted delight in Chaucer. And though Chaucer, with all his satire of ecclesiastics, was a good Catholic, there are few parts of his work where a Catholic reader has an advantage over a non-Catholic. The reasons do not need to be spelled out; it is clear that Chaucer's rich and substantial humanity transcends time and creeds. We might say that, possessing an assured faith which settled all final issues, he was free to focus his genial, unblinking gaze on men and women as they are. Yet that view would hardly explain Dante or the English Dante, Langland, and we must make large allowance for Chaucer's individual temper. And Chaucer was not always content with contemplation of the human comedy. We remember the tragic as well as the comic ironies of *Troilus*, and the moving epilogue in which the poet exhorts young fresh folks to turn from the passions of earth to the security of heavenly love.

For our problem, Dante is of course a supreme test case. Mr. Eliot recommended knowledge and understanding and the suspension of both belief and disbelief — although he brought a great deal more than that to his own reading, as indeed he acknowledged. Mr. Eliot has probably been a principal agent in what may be called a revival of Dante, which seems to have gone on mainly though not wholly among actual or vestigial Christians. It may at any rate be presumed that the secular reader's enjoyment progressively lessens after he leaves the *Inferno*, and that full response to the *Paradiso* is available chiefly to the Christian. I cannot help recalling here the remark of an eminent Christian-Platonist philosopher and sympathetic reader, A. E. Taylor, that for most of us Dante's paradise has, at moments, an unfortunate resemblance to a glorified firework night at the Crystal Palace. If I may, with even more candor, use myself as an ill-starred guinea pig, I must report that, after numerous readings over many years, I still find much of the *Divine Comedy* more alien than Homer and Virgil and

Aeschylus and Sophocles; and I should like to think that my failure is not due entirely to inadequate command of Italian or theology or philosophy or inadequacy of belief. Doctrine that becomes bare and obtrusive may, no doubt, awaken problems of belief that imagination had kept quiescent, yet the exposition of doctrine is not necessarily fatal; beliefs and ideas, passionately felt, can make superb poetry, as in Lucretius or in Milton's passage on the old law and the gospel, which rightly evokes in Mr. Rajan an ecstasy of admiration. Nor, in this as in other cases, is the mere reconstruction of beliefs and ideas an obstacle; all literature of the past necessitates the reconstruction of a multitude of secular data. The question is how far the reasonably informed and well-disposed reader is able to enter into a given work, and no general formula will cover individual instincts and limitations. Since, for an infinity of readers much better equipped than I, Dante is one of the world's greatest poets, a Lilliputian arrow will not damage him, so I will go on to say that I feel a great gap between his miserable and often dehumanized sinners and his vision of divine love and order, and that what is lacking is the ethical humanity that is so central in the classical poets. Those who wish to consign me to the lowest circle of hell are anticipated by my own sentence.

That ethical humanity is central, along with religion, in Spenser, a poet whose fate it has been to be widely misread in the past as a romantic dreamer and picture-maker and in modern times to be read and understood only by scholars. Some readers avoid *The Faerie Queene* altogether because of the allegory, and some follow the romantic prescription of ignoring it, which is equally fatal. Northrop Frye remarks in his *Anatomy of Criticism* (p. 90) that the critic "often urges us to read Spenser and Bunyan . . . for the story alone and let the allegory go, meaning by that that he regards his own type of commentary as more interesting." As for storytelling, Josephine Bennett has justly observed that Spenser should be linked with Dante rather than with the romancers he sometimes imitated, Ariosto and Tasso (though of course his loose texture is closer to them than to Dante's density). It is a commonplace of literary history that all rivers of thought and poetic art flow through Spenser, and, with him as with other great poets, the more one knows the better. Yet most of *The Faerie Queene* is richly intelligible to the attentive reader who has a minimal knowledge of the beliefs, ideas, and attitudes of the Renaissance and the Reformation. The first book, of Holiness, has an archetypal structure and theme; it is linked with the motifs of the quest and the unpromising hero, with the romance and the morality play. As a good Anglican, Spenser was a good Calvinist, but he was first of all a devout and compassionate Christian, and his anti-Catholic Protestantism did not prevent his using Catholic symbols. And while in the second book, of Temperance, Guyon is equipped with Platonic and Aristotelian reason, with the power of moral choice, it is in this classical book only that an angel appears, to protect the exhausted hero. Whatever refinements of insight are provided by the reader's learning, no problem of knowledge or belief comes between him and such lines as

> And is there care in heaven? And is there love
> In heavenly spirits to these creatures bace,
> That may compassion of their evils move?
> There is: else much more wretched were the cace
> Of men, then beasts. . . . (II.viii.I)

It is in this book also that, to follow Professor Woodhouse, the conquest of original sin is achieved, not through the power of natural reason, but through Providence and grace.

Spenser can create a myth with the simplicity of an old wives' tale, or with the allusive obliqueness of *The Waste Land.* Thus at the end of Book I, when St. George, the Knight of Holiness, has slain the dragon of evil, his merging with the figure of Christ is indicated in unmistakable terms:

> And after to his Pallace he them brings,
> With shaumes, and trompets, and with Clarions sweet;
> And all the way the joyous people sings,
> And with their garments strowes the paved street. (I.xii.13)

A more familiar example of the same kind is the beginning of the climactic stanza of the *Epithalamion*:

> Open the temple gates unto my love,
> Open them wide that she may enter in. . . .

Here Spenser suggests both the religious order of marriage and his reverence for his bride through a daring echo of the Twenty-fourth Psalm: "Lift up your heads, O ye gates. And be ye lift up, ye everlasting doors, and the king of glory shall come in." Spenser, by the way, and Milton likewise, differ from the early Eliot and some other modern poets both in not using private allusions and in not putting the whole weight of meaning on an allusion; the allusion is a great enrichment of meaning, but is not the sole clue. For a Miltonic example, when, after Adam has allied himself with Eve in her sin, and she exclaims "O glorious trial of exceeding love," the general irony is clear; but the phrase suggests further the contrast between her selfishness and Adam's weakness and the selfless love of Christ for man.

The case of Milton is partly parallel to Spenser's. Nineteenth-century criticism, in the romantic and liberal tradition, did not understand *Paradise Lost*, and either exalted its author as an unwitting member of the devil's party or ignored his fable and ideas altogether and listened only to the organ voice. In spite of the illuminating activities of modern scholarship and criticism, Miltonic truth is still bestuck with slanderous darts, and *Paradise Lost* has rested under a much heavier handicap than the *Divine Comedy*, though it might seem to possess some advantages. It is a great fable of the never-ending war between good and evil, humility and pride, in the world and in the heart of man; its design is simple and clear as well as vast; the poem moves with energy and speed; it has much less theology and philosophy than the *Divine Comedy*; and if it lacks ordinary human characters (and Adam and Eve become a very human Everyman and Everywoman), it does not require in running footnotes a Who's Who of medieval Europe. If it is said that Dante's style commends itself to modern poets as a model, while Milton's does not, most readers are not poets, and the colloquial is not the only good kind of style; moreover, while old-fashioned critics like Dr. Leavis see Milton as a simple-minded rhetorician splashing at a ten-league canvas with brushes of comets' hair, more discerning students have begun to recognize and analyze the subtleties of Milton's language, syntax, and rhythm — subtleties that are below the surface and were not supposed to exist in "classical" art. Since Dante's beliefs can hardly be more palatable to the modern intellectual than Milton's, and might well be less so, one suspects that some readers simply dislike Milton's personality, or alleged personality (as Mr. Eliot avowedly does), though it is doubtful if Dante's was a very sweet and pliable nature. The same charge attaches to Milton's God, who, though he can speak like a divine being, may be said to reveal a partial failure in poetic tact. Yet it seems a bit strange that a few lines from God, which, though harsh in tone, are a repudiation of Calvinism and an assertion of man's individual responsibility, should antagonize readers who are quite undisturbed by the multitudinous victims and tortures of Dante's hell.

The conventional misinterpretation of *Paradise Lost* has been kept alive partly through the inertia of unenlightened prejudice, partly through the failure to see that Milton's technique is not merely epic but dramatic. He presents characters in the way Shakespeare does, relying, as Shakespeare could rely, on the religious and ethical reactions of his audience, on the religious and ethical absolutes of general acceptance. Shakespeare, to be sure, may leave good at least outwardly defeated by evil, though his audience is left in no doubt as to which is which, and in no real doubt as to the nature of the defeat and the victory. Milton, both because he is Milton and because the epic allows direct comment, is much more positive and explicit. Thus, since evil, whatever its success, cannot ultimately overcome good, Satan and his fellows are enveloped from first to last in irony. A sufficient example is Satan's first speech of defiance, uttered when he finds Beëlzebub beside him in the lake of fire: "If thou beest he — but O how fallen . . ." It is from this speech, and the shorter ones that follow, that romantic misinterpretation starts. Readers who automatically applaud a rebel, no matter what he is, what his motives are, or what he rebels against, see nothing but heroic grandeur in this speech, though every line of its reveals Satan's corruption as plainly as Iago's speeches reveal his; but no one has ever been naive enough to take Iago as Shakespeare's interpreter.

If, in the present age of enlightenment, the Satanist fallacy no longer needs demonstration, Milton can supply a harder test for the non-Christian or even the Christian reader, both of whom may assume that this poet sees everything in crude black and white. After Adam's first chill of horror that follows Eve's blithe account of her sin, he speaks thus:

> O fairest of creation, last and best
> Of all God's works, creature in whom excelled
> Whatever can to sight or thought be formed,
> Holy, divine, good, amiable, or sweet!
> How art thou lost, how on a sudden lost,
> Defaced, deflowered, and now to death devote!
> Rather how hast thou yielded to transgress
> The strict forbiddance, how to violate
> The sacred fruit forbidden! Some cursed fraud
> Of enemy hath beguiled thee, yet unknown,
> And me with thee hath ruined, for with thee
> Certain my resolution is to die;
> How can I live without thee, how forgo
> Thy sweet converse and love so dearly joined,
> To live again in these wild woods forlorn? . . .

We can notice only a couple of things here. The first four lines are an unwitting revelation of the idolatry that will soon lead Adam to share Eve's sin; she is not the "fairest of creation, . . . best / Of all God's works . . ." Eve herself has fallen through seeking to become a goddess, but Adam had already made her one, raising her above himself and hence above his relation to God. In now clinging to Eve in her sin Adam is, as Gerard Manley Hopkins said, falsely chivalrous, though not every reader can wholeheartedly apply Hopkins' Christian scale of values. And Milton himself, in implicitly condemning Adam, makes us at the same time feel and sympathize with his human loyalty. More than one critic has remarked on the poignant power of the lines in which Adam's anguished imagination anticipates Eden, hitherto the perfect paradise, as, without Eve, "these wild woods forlorn."

This rapid survey of some large works seems to lead to the same conclusion as our glance over short religious poems: namely, that, while we may not share the religious creeds of these poets, and while they would not be what they are if they had not held those creeds, their full and enduring appeal to us — artistic power being again taken for granted — depends upon the degree to which their vision of the world and human experience transcends particular articles of belief (and a still more cogent example might have been *Samson Agonistes*). This is, to be sure, only another truism, and one that operates no less in the purely secular sphere; those works that are tied to ephemeral themes, like some plays of Ibsen and Shaw, may fade with the fading of the causes they espoused (unless saved by other elements). But I do not mean that a poet's religious view of the world and human destiny must be reduced by criticism to nonreligious terms, must be purged of its essence, in order that the nonreligious reader may receive only the kind of ideas he prefers or is used to. I mean rather that the religious poet must himself establish enough common ground for them both to stand on. If the secular reader is to gain what may be thought a higher vision than his own, it must come — if we are sticking to literature — through a poet whose vision of perfection embraces also a vision of earth and the natural man, or, to turn things around, through a poet whose vision of earth and the natural man embraces also a vision of perfection. The proportions may of course vary widely — Chaucer and Shakespeare on the one hand, Dante and Milton on the other, and Spenser in the middle — but it is the very definition of the greatest poets, including the ancients, that they have such a simultaneous double vision. To some, Shakespeare may seem a dubious figure here, even on the less overtly religious side;

yet, though we may stop well short of recent pictures of him as a dramatist of positive Christian symbolism, we cannot dispute his continual and significant Christian allusions and overtones. And though it has been said that the least touch of any theology which has a compensating heaven to offer the tragic hero is fatal, it is perhaps legitimate to think, for example, of "And flights of angels sing thee to thy rest."

I linked the ancients with the Christian poets, and they provide impressive confirmation of the argument, if any be needed. In our reading of the Greek and Latin poets, to repeat the obvious, the question of belief does not arise. Yet this body of poetry and drama remains the fountainhead of Western literature and a living possession for us not merely because of artistic greatness but mainly because its ethical values are so largely our values; we apprehend them with a directness that elements of difference cannot obscure. Moreover, while pagan religion and ethics through the centuries underwent a process of refinement not unlike that of Christianity, those ethical standards carried religious as well as human and rational sanctions. Homer's gods may at times be morally irresponsible, or even comic, but they can also guide and protect human virtue. "The blessed gods," says Eumaeus to Odysseus, "do not love wicked deeds but honor justice and the righteous acts of men." Anyhow, whatever the vagaries of the gods, Homer's ethics have an unfailing soundness and rightness. What was instinctive and practical in Homer was, much later, philosophized in the ethical psychology of Plato and, later still, in the Stoic doctrine of right reason. Both that psychology and that doctrine of right reason, which rest on accepted absolutes, were absorbed by Christianity; we may recall that famous utterance of Hooker's which begins with an assertion that may seem, from a devout Christian, rather startling: "The general and perpetual voice of men is as the sentence of God himself. . . ." Thus Christian ethics could operate in one or more of several interrelated ways, in terms of obedience to divine commands, to the conscious ethical reason, or to the instincts of common decency. All three ways are manifest in Shakespeare. If Shakespeare's religious creed is very different from Homer's, and no less his questioning of the human situation, his ethics have the same soundness and rightness. His highroad leading nowhere, as Alfred Harbage has said, is the road home; what he tells us is what we have always known — though he tells us much more too. If his tragedies lacked all Christian motives and coloring, there would be a great loss, yet their center of gravity would not be displaced; they would be inconceivably different, or rather, they would not be conceivable at all, if he were morally neutral or naturalistic.

When the slayer of Hector and the father of Hector meet, brought together by the command of Zeus, they both learn the meaning of compassion. The same lesson is learned, through suffering, by King Lear, and he dies, like the aged Oedipus, in the knowledge of love given and received. The mind of Hamlet swarms with ideas and feelings unknown to Orestes, but there are affinities between them; and if the individual revenger, heaven's scourge and minister, in some sense fails, the health of Denmark is to be restored by Fortinbras as a new kind of justice is established with the Areopagus. In both Aeschylus and Shakespeare, whatever the success of evil in the world, there is a righteous power that catches up with the wicked. And the religious integrity that unites Antigone with Jeanie Deans bridges the gulf between the laws that grow not old and the God of Scottish Calvinism. To go outside religious ethics, a young man's initiation into the adult world of evil links Sophocles'

Neoptolemus with the central figure in Hemingway's *The Killers*. I do not forget the far greater heights and depths of vision and experience that Christianity brought with it, yet, in the spirit of Erasmus' "Sancte Socrates, ora pro nobis," we may say of the greatest pagan and Christian poets that they "are folded in a single party."

Literature

I SHOULD LIKE TO start with a few generalities which suggest some of the conditions of the problem.

First, according to an educational investigator of 1949, one half of the adult population of the United States is "functionally illiterate," that is, unable to read with ordinary comprehension the books and magazines addressed to the general public.[1]

Secondly, the impression that we are not a reading nation was confirmed by a poll — so far as polls are valid — conducted in 1956.[2] At that time only 17 per cent of Americans were found to be reading books, as compared with 31 per cent in Canada, 34 per cent in Australia, and 55 per cent in England; 57 per cent of our high school graduates and 26 per cent of our college graduates had not read a single book during the preceding year; of the college graduates, 9 per cent could not name the author of any one of twelve famous books in English, 39 per cent could not name more than three; and 45 per cent could not name any recently published book.

Reprinted by permission from *The Case for Basic Education: A Program of Aims for Public Schools*, ed. James D. Koerner (Boston: Atlantic-Little, Brown and Company, 1959), © 1959 by Council for Basic Education.

[1] William S. Gray, cited in J. J. De Boer, W. V. Kaulfers, and H. R. Miller, *Teaching Secondary English* (New York, 1951), pp. 161–62, 202.

[2] The poll, conducted by the American Institute of Public Opinion, was reported in *Science*, April 27, 1956.

Thirdly, schoolwork is only part of an adolescent's life, and, even if all schools in the country were perfect (and many are more or less good), they would still be facing heavy odds and could not accomplish miracles.

Fourthly, the mass of the high school population, like the mass of their elders, do not want to read literature new or old; they have other things to do. But the prime concern of this essay — as of other essays in this book — is with good students.

Fifthly, a great many of even the good students are affected by the prevalence of illiteracy. One phenomenon of our age of mass media is that good usage is so widely and quickly corrupted by both unconscious and conscious debasement of diction and idiom.

We cannot wing our way upward into the ideal aims of the study of literature in serene disregard of such brute facts of life, and something must be said here of one of them. We tend to associate illiteracy with writing and speaking, in which it is most glaringly exposed. But along with bad writing goes the incapacity for intelligent reading, which cripples every kind of intellectual activity and is quite fatal in the study of works of literary art. Literacy, in the elementary sense of correctness of expression, ought to be largely achieved in the elementary school; but, as any college teacher knows, a distressing proportion of our college students and graduates are not literate even to this limited degree. While I have no statistics on the matter, when I look back over thirty-five years of teaching I have a strong conviction that illiteracy has grown steadily worse. When I began, it was almost unknown among graduate students in English; now, in varying degrees, it is not uncommon. And one group is, with exceptions, consistently at the foot of the scale in both literacy and critical knowledge of literature — that is, students in Education, the prospective teachers and administrators in our schools.

The causes of illiteracy do not need to be spelled out, though we need to have them in mind if we hope to effect improvement. Reading, the best cure for illiteracy as well as other ills, has suffered from many things that go on outside of school; and we know, from the results, what has happened inside. We are concerned with restoring substance, standards, and discipline, and we must recognize how far pedagogical principles and practice have moved in other directions.

The nearest approach to a bible of orthodoxy on the teaching of literature — because of the number of experts who participated and the number of school systems examined — is two volumes published by the National Council of Teachers of English: the comprehensive survey called *The English Language Arts* (1952) and *The English Language Arts in the Secondary School* (1956) — volumes cited here, for brevity, as *ELA* and *ELASS* respectively. While both books, like others I have read on the teaching of high school English, contain much wisdom on many problems, they also contain much that may be thought unwisdom. To language and literature they apply the familiar "student-centered" doctrines that have made so much of our secondary education what it is. The word "democratic" is an incantation that serves to glorify socially minded ignorance and triviality. Since pupils' abilities and needs differ so widely even within the same grade (democracy presumably puts them in the same grade), the only prescription — surely a very authoritarian prescription — is that every individual should learn what is thought appropriate for him at a given time. A modern program, it is said, must not permit the setting up of minimum essentials or objective standards or the concept of nonpromotion; there is a sufficient incentive in achievement and growth (*ELA*, pp. 189–90).

This doctrine is supposed to be realistic as well as democratic. Illiterate writing and reading and other evils are the inevitable product of schools in which there are no objective standards and in which everyone is promoted regardless of work not done. In recent years, thanks in large part to the campaign waged by only a few persons, a good many laymen and some officials have been awakened. Several years ago the school system of New York City announced the abolishing of automatic promotion, and last spring it did not promote 4000 pupils who showed deficient ability in reading; apparently the sense of growth was not an adequate incentive. It seems clear that schools must strive, through rigorous enforcement of objective standards by literate teachers, to make young people literate. And college teachers in general have not been guiltless; many of them assume that good English concerns the English department, not theirs.

To try to say what a high school student — or anyone — should get from literature is to weave a tissue of clichés. Yet these clichés have for several thousand years been vivid realities, and they become vivid realities whenever a reader discovers a new world of imaginative or intellectual experience. (I assume that my topic means imaginative art, not history, biography, philosophy, and such things.) Literature deals with man in every relation, with the whole texture of outward and inward life, with joys and sorrows, moral defeats and victories, comedy and tragedy, with everything human, in short, and also with mysteries beyond human comprehension. Every serious work of art, from a springtime lyric to an epic, is not only an interpretation of life, it is a part of life. The young — or the old — who openly or tacitly declare that they prefer living to reading are not really living; they exist on a subhuman level, imprisoned in their own meager experience and the passing moment, instead of participating in the life of the whole past and present in all its richness, variety, and intensity. Such participation is directly imaginative and emotional, and it has less direct but not less potent effects that are social, political, psychological, aesthetic, ethical, metaphysical, religious.

Most of what I have just said may suggest an initial and elementary response to literature, one that may be only an uncritical devouring of vicarious experience, and that is quite as it should be with very young readers. But this widening and deepening of individual experience, this imaginative participation in the joys and struggles and crises of the human spirit, is also central in the final response of maturity. We might recall that saying about *Don Quixote* — that in youth it seems a comedy, in middle age a tragedy, and in old age a comedy again. The comedy seen by old age is far richer and more poignant than the comedy seen by youth, but that is not a reason for postponing this and other great books until retirement. The young can become mature only by getting as much as they can out of books at their own time of life; they will get more later — if they do not stop reading. Youthful idealism, whatever it misses, is a dynamic motive that can be turned to great account, and that should not be satisfied or stultified by low-grade books or by versions of classics that abridge and debase them to scenarios for those who read with their lips.

The enlargement of experience, however central, will be very defective unless it includes other motives and assets.

Some of these come with growing up; some are intellectual acquisitions that must be worked for and cultivated. What a person gets from reading depends upon what he brings to it; and no high school pupils have the right to be so ignorant of everything as the pedagogical experts have evidently found the mass of them to be. I have spoken already of elementary literacy and need not return to that. But literacy has larger meanings. One element is knowledge, of which we never have enough for reading masterpieces. No book is so central in the culture of the English-speaking world, no book is so constantly echoed, as the King James Bible (to speak of it only in cultural terms), and no great book seems to be less familiar to the modern high school student, or, for that matter, the college student. No one who has the conceptions, the language, and the rhythms of the Bible in his head can be taken in by the cheap and tawdry. An almost equally unfamiliar treasury of major themes and symbols is Greek and Roman mythology. From Chaucer down through Yeats and Eliot, not to mention the ancients and foreign writers, these themes and symbols are everywhere, and yet every textbook for school and college has to explain the commonest allusion. To take a very simple instance, according to a good book on the teaching of English,[3] the first twenty lines of *L'Allegro* have ten allusions, to *Cerberus*, *Stygian*, and the like, which are more or less beyond the average high school senior. Obviously no one in such Stygian darkness can have much understanding enjoyment.

The study of foreign languages, modern as well as ancient, has for many years been so successfully opposed that a great many American high schools now offer no foreign

[3] Julius N. Hook, *The Teaching of High School English* (New York, 1950), p. 199.

language whatever, and a great many more offer only two years of a language — an all but useless amount. This movement went on during the period in which the United States engaged in three foreign wars and became the leader of the free world. In very recent years international politics have aroused a portion of the public and even the government to our linguistic deficiencies, and the Modern Language Association has carried on an active campaign. It is, too, increasingly recognized that modern languages can and should be painlessly acquired in the elementary grades. But political and utilitarian reasons for a speaking command of everyday language are not enough for cultural purposes — or even for the political understanding of other peoples. It could be earnestly wished that our statesmen would now and then read some literature.

The ancient languages have of course met special hostility for generations. Greek is presumably taught in almost no public school; a small percentage of students take Latin for two years. Against Greek and Latin there is the general charge of uselessness, and, in regard to both them and modern languages, there is the common fallacy that everything, or everything important, has been translated. If the conveyance of ideas is all that matters, a translation — say of Aristotle — is adequate. But if writers, especially poets and dramatists, are great artists in language, only an artist of comparable power can produce a translation — and then it will probably become a quite different work. However, necessity compels general reliance upon translations for both school and college.

It may seem utopian, though it should not, to ask that the upper section of high school students should have a working knowledge of two foreign languages, of which I would say that one should be Latin. And the usual two years are not enough to take students beyond grammar and Caesar; they ought to read Virgil and one or two of the shorter philosophical works of Cicero and other things. If Virgil, the poetic voice of Roman civilization, goes without saying, it may be remembered that Cicero probably had more influence on the Western world than any other writer outside the Bible. Latin is a door to literature and civilization, not a wall of paradigms; it is also a safeguard against some current illiteracy. In general, while many people object to the study of Latin, and while I am not of course proposing it for all students, I believe firmly that it should be amply available for good students and that they should be encouraged to take it — and a great many enjoy it when they do.

Although *ELA* and *ELASS* often urge the social, inspirational, and aesthetic value of literature, one is left uncertain and uneasy, amid all the planning and all the machinery, about the actual place of real literature in school.[3a] And while it is assumed that students will read some of the older literature — the ballads, Shakespeare, Milton, and so on — the whole program in "communication" seems to be directed toward the use of the spoken language of the present moment in the United States. The result of such emphasis is that the language of Shakespeare and Milton becomes a foreign language. I have already cited a pedagogical expert (who is following another expert) [4] on the difficulties of *L'Allegro*: it has not only classical allusions but, they say, strange words like *hamlet* and *haycock*, which the

[3a] See the survey of high school textbooks in English by Lynch and Evans (1963) cited below under "The Humanities," note 2.

[4] Klise S. King, "Vocabulary Difficulties in Poetry," *English Journal*, XXX (1941), 36–41, cited in Hook, p. 199.

student confuses with *hammock* and a bird that lives in the hay. Students who are, by life and instruction, immersed in mass media and the idiom of the street, and who have set before them the ideals of "general social acceptance and business success," [5] are not likely to respond to the grand affirmation:

> We must be free or die, who speak the tongue
> That Shakespeare spake; the faith and morals hold
> Which Milton held.

The aims set forth in *ELA* and *ELASS* in part agree with those in the short but excellent discussion of literature in *General Education in School and College*,[6] but the former represent the public school and the latter the private, and there is a difference in the level of aims and assumptions. In various books by educational experts about high school English one may be depressed, for instance, by the elaborate devices suggested for luring indifferent or hostile students into reading. This may be the lesson of painful experience, and reading must above all be enjoyed, in some fashion. But response to literature may be cramped and warped by excessive concern with the student's own little world and with social adjustment. Thus in one book we are told that social sensitivity, a delicate respect for others, "is what we learn from literature." [7] However desirable that virtue, it is surely not in that spirit that we read Homer and the *Oresteia* and *King Lear* and *Paradise Lost*. So, too, *ELA*, although it gives (p. 391) a wise warning against making literature the mere tool of social studies, seems to

[5] *ELA*, p. 295.

[6] *General Education in School and College: A Committee Report by Members of the Faculties of Andover, Exeter, Lawrenceville, Harvard, Princeton, and Yale* (Cambridge, Mass., 1953).

[7] De Boer, Kaulfers, and Miller, *Teaching Secondary English*, p. 211.

approach it very much in that way. After reading about "units" on "In and Out of Family Living" and "Making the Most of Oneself," one has visions of preparing for *Hamlet* by way of units on "The Stepfather in the Home" and "Disillusionment with a Date." Such approaches to literature may be necessitated by the endeavor to penetrate crass obtuseness, but they ought to be needless on higher levels. A young child does not have to be led by a devious route into fairy tales; why should an adolescent be socially processed before reading more advanced prose and poetry? And why, the schoolteacher may wonder, with dismay, does the eager interest of the first-grader so often become the bored indifference of the high school freshman? While any good curriculum will take young readers from the simple to the complex, can they move up from social trivia, or even social virtues, to the study of great art? No matter how immature adolescents actually are, they will not become mature unless they are treated as if they were so; and the world of great literature is something more than an extension of the world of school life.

But a major sin of modern education, in all branches of the curriculum, has been the unwillingness to demand serious effort. An odd revelation of what constitutes an intellectual giant appears in *ELA* (p. 243): "It has been reported that a college student reads from six to twelve books a year as a part of his regular course. This in itself is no mean accomplishment. . . ." In literature, as in everything else, even the feeblest minds need to be stretched; and there is far greater need for stretching the better minds, which can enjoy a sense of growth, the exhilaration of a problem solved, an illuminating insight gained. That means, not a regimen of unrelaxed austerity — much of the world's best writing, especially in English literature, is pure humor and comedy — but a considerable proportion of works beyond the reader's normal reach. Such works may be assigned or may be hit upon in independent reading; occasional ventures may be premature, but for active readers the excited enjoyment of their own discoveries may be a new birth. (I remember my own schoolboy passion for Macaulay, which led me to read everything he wrote, and which inspired a better passion for Burke.) Last summer, as a tiny bit of field work in connection with this paper, members of a college class in composition were asked to name a book that had stirred them in high school; most of the authors were good, though they ranged from Homer and Tolstoy to Sabatini and Zane Grey. Everyone, young or old, reads a great deal of minor or mediocre writing, or sheer trash, but even the fairly young should have enough discrimination to know what kind of thing they are reading.

ELA and *ELASS* insist, as I have said, that reading must be appropriate to the individual learner's stage of growth. Since high school students cannot be taught individually, such a principle, whatever its degree of intrinsic wisdom, seems unrealistic; and the repudiation of objective standards is likely to leave one tacit standard, the lowest common denominator. As *ELA* says, a good many of the young are incapable of reading the literary classics; perhaps they have to be left to fraternize with Tarzan — or whoever the current hero may be. But for the large body of students a mixed and flexible list of authors and books may well be set up as a normal goal; in the educational books cited, however, suggested lists of reading mix the great with the little or the negligible in a quite puzzling way — for instance, "*Sorrell and Son*, *Hamlet*, and *Antigone*" (*ELASS*, p. 139). As for those who are going to college, or are of college caliber (the two groups are not identical), the college teacher has a right to expect that he will have a fairly broad and solid foundation to build on. One well-founded conviction that runs through the essays in this book is that our high schools have set their sights far too low. In literature, as in other subjects, the high school diploma should represent a measure of positive achievement and not simply attendance. To have made good headway in the art of reading is something; but the able high school graduate should also, through assigned and voluntary reading, have some substantial knowledge.

While the mass of English literature is so large that one hesitates to suggest names, it would seem reasonable that the better high school graduates should know some of the popular ballads, four or five plays of Shakespeare, the chief minor poems of Milton, and some poems by at least half a dozen of the other major English poets; representative novels, unabridged, by half a dozen of the major novelists (and not merely *Ivanhoe*, *A Tale of Two Cities*, and *Silas Marner*, if these are still staples); and some miscellaneous things from *Pilgrim's Progress* to Burke's *On Conciliation with America*. If such a modest proposal evokes outcries, I can only echo a saying of Billy Sunday: "They say I rub people's fur the wrong way; I say, 'Let the cats turn around.' "

ELA reflects a general movement in approving of the reduction of reading in British literature and the enlargement of that in American and contemporary authors. There was, to be sure, a time when American literature was denied its rightful place in both school and college; and it is essential that high school graduates should know something of the dozen chief writers of the nineteenth century and some modern ones. But it is equally essential that they should not develop a merely national and provincial outlook and scale of values. American democracy — the theme song of so many books on education — has deep British and European roots, and, anyhow, it is not the sole and perfect end for which the world was made. No American writers are among the world's greatest, and the young need to experience the greatest; great poetry in particular must be studied in a language one knows, and very little great poetry has been written in the United States in comparison with that of England. Lionel Trilling had what may be thought a disturbing address in the *Sewanee Review*, in the summer of 1958, on the loss American education increasingly suffers through its increasing movement away from British literature, the literature which is our common heritage, which is infinitely richer than American, which has many elements that we need to absorb, and which, in its comprehensive and coherent pattern, is the one literature in our own language that can be systematically studied.

According to pedagogical books and articles, the newer courses in world literature appear to be in high and growing favor, perhaps because, on paper, they build "community consciousness" on a grand scale. Any such course in school is bound to be spotty and thin. A very few works, read with care and due consideration of their background, are much better than the skimming of many fragmentary selections. For instance, Greece might be represented by the *Odyssey*, *Oedipus Rex*, Plato's *Apology* (and, if possible, the *Republic*), Aristotle's *Poetics*, and, in North's translation, Plutarch's life of one of Shakespeare's heroes. A minimal knowledge of Latin literature, in Latin, has already been spoken of. It was, by the way, a favorite prejudice of John Dewey that ancient literature was the product of slave-holding nations; we might remember that all the American writers of the golden age were likewise citizens of a slave-holding nation, the latest in the modern world. Some modern foreign authors will be read in one or other of the modern languages. It might be hoped that voluntary reading would include one or two Russian novels, in translation.

It is a question how far high school students should be taken into the historical study of literature, whether British and American or foreign. For the average student, probably historical significance and continuity must, if reckoned with at all, be kept to a minimum. But the abler students would surely gain a good deal from a relatively consecutive and philosophical view of the evolution and interrelations of literature and ideas and the state of civilization. Overemphasis on the contemporary means a fatal lack of perspective and taste.

A high school senior can and should develop some capacity for the critical and technical analysis of a novel, a play, or a poem. Impressionistic gush is not a substitute for rational understanding of the elements and problems of imaginative art, of structure and texture and tone; such understanding of course enriches and refines enjoyment. One branch of technique of which students seem to know little is metrics, though such knowledge is essential for the reading of poetry old or new. And, thinking of the supreme importance of rhythm, one may add that the oral reading of poetry — by the old as well as the young — can often torture the sensitive ear.

For both the gifted and the average, however, the primary response to literature is, and should be, ethical and aesthetic rather than historical or technical. Young readers, and old ones, are moved chiefly by a writer's view of life. Moreover, while for many people literature is the most attractive study this world affords, it demands, more than other kinds of material, teachers above the common level. There have been, and there are, a good many of these, but they are few in relation to the need.

By way of conclusion, I may perhaps be allowed to fall back on some sentences of my own from another discourse, since they sum up the chief claims and rewards of literature as well as I am able to do it. From antiquity until recent times, literature has been the main medium of education, and, in spite of — or because of — the emergence of new kinds of knowledge, its responsibilities have not shrunk. They have indeed grown more important than ever, as many things have combined to lower the dignity, benumb the sensibility, and drown the voice of individual man. The aim of the humanities, of literature, is not to adjust people to life, to the values of mass civilization, but to enlighten and disturb them, to inspire and strengthen them to adjust life and themselves to the traditional ideals of the best minds, the saving remnant of the human race. Modern literature, the literature of the age of anxiety, has been preoccupied with man's increasing consciousness of his loss of outward and inward wholeness and order, with his sense of being a fragment in a fragmentary world. And the eternal quest of literature, intensified by the common modern loss of religious assurance, has been the quest of order. From the chaos of life and society the artist seeks a pattern of explanation, a pattern that enables him and his readers to achieve some measure of dominion over experience. In literature ethical and aesthetic values are inseparably bound up together. The great instrument of moral good, said Shelley, is the imagination; and poetry administers to the effect by acting upon the cause. In literature students find, as countless people have found before them, that their problems are not new; and they may find also that writers of an earlier day had answers that are not out of date but richly worth pondering. Literature of the remote past as well as the present contains what is not contained in textbooks of psychology and sociology and science, the vision of human experience achieved by a great spirit and bodied forth by a great artist. The great artist's vision of life is not dimmed or deadened by time because it is a distillation of man's finest insights, of his supreme awareness of what man is and of what man might be. Thus the literature of the centuries of ancient paganism, of the centuries of Christianity, and of our own era, the era some call post-Christian, all this constitutes a simultaneous and living whole. The great writers, pagan, Christian, agnostic, with all their differences, "are folded in a single party"; they are the imagination and the conscience of mankind.

Science and Literature in the Seventeenth Century

DURING THE NINETEENTH CENTURY the great watershed between the medieval and the modern era was commonly taken to be the Renaissance of the fifteenth and sixteenth centuries. In our time the watershed has been moved up to the seventeenth-century "Enlightenment." In this large change of focus the history of science has played a large role.

Professor Toulmin has suggestively outlined the complex effects of the scientific revolution upon the humanities. In dealing with literature one would need, even if one were writing a book instead of an essay, to begin with some provisos. First, since the body of significant English literature is itself far too big to cope with, one cannot bring in Continental as well; but, so far as my knowledge goes, no national literature of the Continent surpasses English in its responsiveness to science. Secondly, although science was one important factor in the distinctive change of style in prose and verse, we shall be looking mainly at the basic effects on belief and thought and sensibility of which style is the outward manifestation. Thirdly, while science is our

Reprinted by permission from *Seventeenth Century Science and the Arts*, ed. Hedley H. Rhys (Princeton, 1961), © 1961 by Princeton University Press. The bibliography accompanying the essay has not been included here.

theme, we should never forget that old certitudes were being undermined by other powerful forces, from the Reformation and sectarian divisions to the revival of ancient philosophic skepticism, along with the problems that afflict people in every age. Finally, though we cannot avoid generalizing about tendencies and attitudes, all generalities must be understood as limited and qualified. We cannot talk about "the seventeenth-century mind" any more than we can about "the twentieth-century mind," since in any period such a label covers a wide spectrum of variations. (I might add that I shall never, except now, use the word "baroque.") Moreover, within an individual mind of the seventeenth — or the twentieth — century there normally coexist beliefs and attitudes, old and new, which to posterity appear incompatible; two eminent exemplars of such mixtures are Bacon and Descartes, and a list would include almost every scientist and thinker and writer as well as the crowd of men in the street.

From the mid-sixteenth century onward, English scientists and mathematicians were, in their number, genius, and variety of achievement, a conspicuous part of the European vanguard; the more or less illustrious names run from Robert Recorde, John Dee, Thomas Digges, Thomas Harriot, William Gilbert, John Napier, William Harvey, and Bacon up to Robert Boyle, Robert Hooke, John Ray, and Sir Isaac Newton. Latin was still the international language, so that there was osmosis, public and private, between English and Continental scientists. Along with experiment and speculation of all kinds, the telescope and later the microscope immensely enlarged the range of observation; some old notions were killed and some new ones established. Behind the manifold discoveries in celestial and terrestrial nature were diverse motives. One was the pressure of technological needs in everyday work and production, from mining to navigation. Another was the shift of inquiry from final to secondary causes, from the metaphysical and religious question "Why?" to the scientific question "How?" — from abstract theory to measurement. That shift, we may remember, had been made by a number of minds in the later Middle Ages.

Seventeenth-century England yielded a large bulk of more or less scientific writing that is more or less important in the history of ideas, but none of it belongs to great literature except that of Bacon (and Burton, if we count him as a scientist). Though Bacon did not of course invent experimentation, he was the herald and prophet of the experimental method and the gospel of scientific and technological progress. *The Advancement of Learning* (1605) is such a landmark, such a majestic *Summa*, in intellectual history, and such a monument of English prose, that a few things must be said about it. While physical science was only one major area in Bacon's stocktaking of the whole field of knowledge, his general criteria were those of a scientific positivist. The three chief "vanities" of learning that have hindered progress — literary and stylistic education, scholastic logic, and such pseudo-sciences as astrology and alchemy — receive the censure of a Jacobean John Dewey (though Bacon's prose is far from Dewey's). His condescending view of most poetry as escapist fantasy has been that of a good many later scientists and philosophers. History and ethics likewise need to be realistic; Machiavelli has set the wholesome example of showing what men do, not what they ought to do. Passages in the *Advancement* give concrete clues to the purpose of Bacon's essays, most of which were still to come: these would supply the lack of realistic psychological studies of the behavior of men of affairs. Finally, science has been confused and misguided, ever since Plato, by being mixed with theology, and the two realms of knowledge and faith must be kept separate; while Bacon was, according to his light, a good Christian, his concern here and elsewhere seems to be the protection and progress of science, which is more in danger than religion. In all this critical, empirical realism we see the beginnings of the temper that was in no long time to dominate thought and literature.

Bacon also urged the need of plain, precise writing in scientific exposition, and in this as in other things he was to be followed by the Royal Society. But when he wrote the *Advancement* and a number of other philosophic works, and the *Essays*, he was not rigidly bound by such principles. If we compare his writing with that of Gilbert or Harvey or later scientists, we find less scientific bareness than massive plenitude and a figurative, even a poetic, strain.

Bacon's place in the history of scientific thought is too well known to need discussion, though he has suffered a good deal from wrongheaded and repetitive disparagement. At any rate both English and Continental scientists of his century paid full tribute not only to his leadership and inspiring program but to his grasp of scientific method. (One dissenter was his personal physician, Dr. Harvey.) However, while Bacon was a great seminal mind and a great master of prose, it is clear that his philosophic writings exist for us only or mainly as documents in intellectual history — whereas Sir Thomas Browne, with all his aberrations, we read and cherish as a living classic.

Whether or not the young Milton had yet read Bacon, his last public speech at Cambridge (1631–32?) was in part an ardent Baconian vision of man's achieving godlike control of the forces of nature. Abraham Cowley, who had made a name as a metaphysical lyrist of love, in an unfinished epic on King David planted a Baconian college in ancient Judea. But the conspicuous heirs of Bacon were the members of the Royal Society, who were creating a "Salomon's House," an institute of cooperative research, in the spirit of *The New Atlantis.* Some of the founders began to meet about 1645, during the civil war, though the Society was not formally organized until 1662. In the Restoration period it included working scientists and amateurs and men like Pepys and Evelyn and Dryden — a reminder that science had come to be a serious and fashionable interest of laymen. Cowley's ode *To the Royal Society* saluted Bacon, in a fitting and famous figure, as the Moses who had led mankind to the edge of the promised land. For a general testimony to the ever-growing consciousness of progress we might quote such a pure man of letters as Dryden (*Essay of Dramatic Poesy*, 1668):

> Is it not evident, in these last hundred years (when the Study of Philosophy has been the business of all the Virtuosi in Christendome), that almost a new Nature has been reveal'd to us? that more errours of the School have been detected, more useful Experiments in Philosophy have been made, more Noble Secrets in Opticks, Medicine, Anatomy, Astronomy, discover'd, than in all those credulous and doting Ages from Aristotle to us? so true it is, that nothing spreads more fast than Science, when rightly and generally cultivated.

Along with Dryden's well-founded testimony to progress we might recall a book that illustrates a not untypical blend of old and new, Sir Thomas Browne's *Pseudodoxia Epidemica* or *Vulgar Errors*, which first appeared in 1646 and had revised editions beyond the date of Dryden's *Essay*. In Browne's opening account of the common causes of error the Baconian critical spirit is mixed with Brownesque piety and antiquarianism. In most of the work he was providing what Bacon had called for, a natural history that would sift truth from the traditional lore of centuries, and he used observation and experiment when he could. When he could not, he weighed reason and authority, as in proving that elephants' legs have joints; we may be further surprised by the reasoning brought to bear on the supposed inequality of a badger's legs. Browne was in many respects a true and zealous scientist — he had had the best medical training Europe afforded, and he thought Harvey a greater discoverer than Columbus — but the reverent wonder that inspires his finest writing is more religious than scientific. Most of his problems do not, as many of Bacon's and the Royal Society's do, look forward to the industrial revolution, though the *Pseudodoxia* is much more inviting than most of the books that propagated the gospel of science and progress, such as Sprat's *History of the Royal Society* (1667).

With full recognition of the rapid growth and dazzling achievements of science in the seventeenth century, we must keep in mind our proper subject, literature; and a good deal of that was less optimistic than the literature of science, for its serious authors seldom forgot man's fallen state, from which science would not raise him.

Throughout the century the strongest impact on thought and literature came from astronomy and cosmology, and we shall follow that main line. But first we may glance at the pseudo-sciences of alchemy and astrology which Bacon had put among the chief obstacles in the way of true science, and which had indeed a marked revival in Europe in the sixteenth and the early seventeenth centuries. They illustrate the twilight that hovers over man's transition from the old world of the mind to the new, and also the quite legitimate way in which — in the spirit of alchemy — living metaphors might emerge from dead bodies of science.

The quest of the philosopher's stone, which could transform the baser metals into gold, had been laughed at by Chaucer, and it could be used by Ben Jonson for one of his satirical exposures of knavery and greed. An agent for transmuting metals, a magical elixir for bodily ills, and, on higher levels, a religious creed of cloudy mysticism — these ideas were still alive, but they had largely given way to genuine chemistry, at first as the rational search for new medical drugs and then in its broad modern sense. On the scientific side it may be added that alchemy had been a real "prelude to chemistry," and that the notion of transmuting elements could rightly attract scientific minds from Bacon to Boyle and Newton; a partly similar idea has been a reality for modern science. A second point, closer to our present concern, is that both the basic principle and its offshoots grew out of the universal belief in the divine unity of the whole creation. Thirdly, the old occult notions continued to yield abundant images and metaphors which had their own imaginative and emotional validity.

An example of the simplest kind might be Shakespeare's glorious morning "Gilding pale streams with heavenly alchemy." But "scientific" complexity fills a passage near the end of Book III of *Paradise Lost* where Satan's alighting on the sun leads Milton to gather up all that man had ever thought and felt about the source of light and life. In his description of the alchemists' vain endeavors — which, Kester Svendsen remarks, carries a judgment on self-deceiving pride akin to Satan's — the main ideas come through to the uninformed reader, as they usually do in Milton's technical passages, with almost unimpaired force and with a touch of suggestive mystery. But Donne's *Nocturnall upon S. Lucies Day*, while it tells the uninformed reader that the poet feels annihilated by grief, has a texture that is hardly intelligible without knowledge of alchemical and especially Paracelsian doctrines. Of all poets of the century, Donne had the most up-to-date stock of scientific information; he was also the most addicted to alchemical language and images, though seldom with the sustained density we have in this poem.

Our second pseudo-science, astrology, was, as Kepler said, the foolish little daughter of the respectable, reasonable mother, astronomy; yet Kepler, the great mathematical lawgiver of early modern astronomy, not only was an astrologer himself but associated ideas of the Trinity with the solar system. While in England many condemned judicial or prophetic astrology as spurious or sinful, it was the common moderate view that the stars exerted an influence upon terrestrial nature and the constitution and hence the destiny of man; in Robert Burton's phrase, the stars "do incline, but not compel." Here again, age-old ideas and metaphors attended and outlived positive belief. The young Milton saw animate Nature awaiting the incarnation of her Creator, the stars "Bending one way their pretious influence"; the old Milton, picturing the effects of man's sin upon nature, described the "noxious efficacie" of planetary motions and aspects and the "influence malignant" of the stars. Andrew Marvell could give astrology a high tragic ring:

> Therefore the Love which us doth bind,
> But Fate so enviously debarrs,
> Is the Conjunction of the Mind,
> And Opposition of the Stars.

Along with astrology may be mentioned the general

belief in natural portents, meteors, comets, eclipses, which, like astrology, is common in Shakespeare, and which inspires that grandly ominous simile in Milton where the sun

> from behind the Moon
> In dim Eclips disastrous twilight sheds
> On half the Nations, and with fear of change
> Perplexes Monarchs.

We may recall here too the Pythagorean-Platonic notion of the music of the spheres, which was evidently as familiar to an Elizabethan theatre audience as less beautiful Freudian ideas are now, since the most famous allusion is in the moonlight dialogue of Lorenzo and Jessica:

> There's not the smallest orb which thou behold'st
> But in his motion like an angel sings,
> Still quiring to the young-ey'd cherubins;
> Such harmony is in immortal souls;
> But, whilst this muddy vesture of decay
> Doth grossly close it in, we cannot hear it.

To take another bifocal glance at Milton, in the *Nativity* the music of the spheres is linked with the music of the angels as a symbol of cosmic harmony; and in *Paradise Lost* the poet is kindled to half-mystical rapture by the more astronomical image of the starry dance, the irregular regularity of the planetary orbits.

Before we ask how the new astronomy affected the seventeenth century, we must ask what was there to be affected, what traditional ways of belief, thought, and feeling constituted the normal world view. That world view has been so often described in recent years that an oversimplified summary will serve. In the Aristotelian-Ptolemaic cosmos the central, stationary earth was surrounded by layers of the other three elements, water, air, and fire; outside these were the spheres of the moon, Mercury, Venus, the sun, Mars, Jupiter, Saturn, and the eighth sphere of fixed stars, all being kept in motion by an outermost ninth or tenth sphere, the *primum mobile*. This and all that went with it were founded on Christian belief in the unity and order of the whole creation. The world of nature, from the spheres to the seasons, operates under the reign of law, divine, prescientific law. It was created to minister to man, and the vast firmament revolves about the earth to give him light and darkness — "The starres," says George Herbert, "have us to bed." The great chain of being descends from God through angels, man, animals, plants, and non-growing matter. All creatures and things have their place in the grand hierarchical pattern, from the classes of angels and of society to the rational and irrational faculties of man's mind. Man, occupying a station midway between the beasts and the angels, is pulled both downward and upward by the warring elements in his own nature. As a being of mind and body, he is the microcosmic parallel to God and the universe. "I am a little world made cunningly," says Donne, "Of Elements, and an Angelike spright"; and Ralegh in his *History of the World* and Donne in his *Devotions* (Meditation iv) draw out the likenesses between man's veins and rivers, and so on. All creatures and things and ideas in the world are linked with one another by analogy and correspondence. In reading metaphysical and other poetry we are often more surprised than we should be at the yoking together of apparently unrelated things; they were not unrelated. And finally as well as first, man and his world are God's creation and under His immediate and providential governance; man's life on earth is only a prelude to eternal bliss or torment. We may remember the two lines that follow the two just quoted from Donne's sonnet:

But black sinne hath betraid to endlesse night
My worlds both parts, and (oh) both parts must die.

Even on earth man is surrounded by good and evil spirits, the ministers of God and Satan; Burton describes both kinds, but only the good are known to Milton's innocent Adam:

Millions of spiritual Creatures walk the Earth
Unseen, both when we wake, and when we sleep.

This classical-Christian world picture had been built up over many centuries, out of traditional philosophy, religion, and the senses and imagination; and, at least in its prime essentials, it was shared by learned and unlearned alike, by Hooker and by Shakespeare. Man could be bestial more often than angelic, but he was God's creature in a world rich in meaning. He knew, if he did not always remember, that he was daily enacting under the divine eye the supreme drama of salvation or damnation. Everyday life was a variegated web of the brutal and the miraculous. To stress only one thing, it was an ideal world for the writer, the poet, a world of crude, harsh, and tragic actuality enveloped in religion and myth and "magic"; human experience and language and image and symbol comprehended the widest and deepest range of significance and contrast. It is no wonder that the late sixteenth and the earlier seventeenth century were the golden age of English poetry and prose. For one of countless reminders, there is Sir Thomas Browne, who, though a scientist, is a superb mid-century exemplar of the old religious and symbolic conceptions of God, nature, and man. *Urn-Burial* and *The Garden of Cyrus* (1658) are, as F. L. Huntley has shown, twin meditations, intersecting circles. The funeral urn has the shape of the womb, and death is "the Lucina of life." Browne's Christian-Platonic imagination works out the parallels and contrasts between death and life, body and soul, matter and form, time and space; these and other opposed concepts come together only in the mind of God, in Eternity and Unity, where darkness and light are one. When we read such things, in language and rhythms that only Browne can command, we may feel that his vision has more reality than all the measurements of the new physics, which belonged to another dimension than the "mysticall Mathematicks of the City of Heaven." Browne's is the world of natural and supernatural order and process, of analogy and "myth" and hieroglyphic — and a large part of our subject here is what Marjorie Nicolson has called "the breaking of the circle."

It took well over a century for the Copernican theory, in spite of the work of Kepler, Galileo, and Elizabethan experts, to win full acceptance even among the learned. In 1643, exactly a hundred years after Copernicus' book, Browne the scientist named the moving of the earth among manifest impossibilities — though his considered position was a not unscientific agnosticism. The reasons for retarded victory were natural. Many learned as well as unlearned men resisted contradiction of the senses and the Bible or of Aristotle, Ptolemy, and all tradition. Many were simply unaware or indifferent, as most of us felt no acute concern over Einstein's discoveries. In both cases few had the mathematical knowledge needed for comprehension or confirmation; indeed the knowledge needed to confirm Copernicus was not fully available until Newton. Also, while Ptolemy "saved the appearances" no less, though less neatly, than Copernicus, the latter in the seventeenth century had a stronger rival in the theory developed by the first great modern observer, the Danish Tycho

Brahe, a compromise which attracted men not quite ready to swallow Copernicus. According to this theory, the earth remained the stationary center of the orbits of the moon, sun, and sphere of fixed stars, and the five planets revolved about the revolving sun. For example, Donne seems to have been a Tychonist; at any rate, though he was well aware of Copernicus, Kepler, and Galileo, he commonly alluded, even in his later verse and prose, to a moving sun and motionless earth. Milton indicated knowledge of the Copernican — not of the Tychonic — system but used the Aristotelian-Ptolemaic one (which was only a small bit of his imagined universe), presumably because he was uncertain, because it was the familiar conception, and because it kept earth and man at the focal center of the cosmic scene. But Milton was of the new age in his imaginative rendering of immense space.

When we consider, abstractly, the effect on thought and literature of the Copernican view of the world, we are likely to slip into fallacious exaggeration. It is often said that the dislodging of the earth from its central place in a comfortably ordered system to the status of a minor planet in vaster space was a fatal blow to man's sense of his own dignity, of his prime rank in creation. This idea, as R. G. Collingwood says, is philosophically foolish and historically false. Throughout the Middle Ages, even though man was the uniquely endowed child of God, the earth was regarded as the basest part of creation. Copernicus himself was no cosmic iconoclast; he was only looking for a simpler pattern of the heavens than Ptolemy's, and he found it. When Thomas Digges, the Elizabethan Copernican, contemplating a universe he saw as infinite, speaks of "this little darcke starre wherein we live," we expect him to continue in the vein of, say, Thomas Hardy or Bertrand Russell; but, for

Digges, the enlargement of the universe only enlarges the glory of its Creator and does not degrade man. And this general attitude persisted among scientists, such as the earnestly religious Boyle and Newton, who upheld God's continuous control of the cosmic order. Indeed, a number of the lesser Copernicans were clergymen, for example, John Wilkins, a champion of the new science and the moving spirit in the formation of the Royal Society. When the moral poet Samuel Daniel, or the physician-lyrist-composer Thomas Campion, or the religious poet George Herbert, or Sir Thomas Browne referred to the earth as a mere point in space (as many others had done, from Cicero and Boethius onward) it was to illustrate the greatness of man's mind, or mutability, or patience in affliction, or some other lesson as old as thought. Shakespeare, if aware of the new astronomy, seems to have been wholly indifferent; and knowledge could hardly have enriched his power over word and rhythm or deepened his insight into human experience, unless perhaps it might have added a cosmic shiver to Hamlet's questionings. But as everyone knows, Hamlet, apart from his private griefs, recognizes the glory of earth and man; and Ulysses' speech in *Troilus and Cressida* (I. iii) is the poetical *locus classicus* for the doctrine of order and degree in the great chain of being.

The Copernican theory seems to have been less disquieting than other discoveries and ideas that were launched or revived along with the new astronomy. Gilbert's argument for the daily rotation of the magnetic earth on its axis received ready scientific approval. But the appearance of new stars in 1572 and 1604 and Galileo's telescopic observations were concrete facts which contradicted the Aristotelian-Christian belief that, whereas the region below the moon was subject to change, the ethereal region beyond was immutable. Yet the old conception lived on as a symbol at least of purity and stability above earthly flux. Donne contrasted the bond between himself and his wife with "Dull sublunary lovers love," a thing of sense, and Sir Thomas Browne, reflecting on the vanity of earthly monuments, saw no "hope for Immortality, or any patent from oblivion, in preservations below the Moon."

Then there was the revived idea of a plurality of inhabited worlds, an idea that intoxicated Giordano Bruno, and later Henry More, but might disturb others. In the most elaborate contemporary survey of astronomical and cosmological theories, in the *Anatomy of Melancholy*, Robert Burton includes the question whether people in other worlds would have souls to be saved. Yet the devout Burton, though deeply compassionate for the varied sufferings of man, seems to be less troubled than amused by astronomy; the thousand bewildering questions will be answered in God's good time. Donne, in his earliest extant sermon, declares that "one of our souls is worth more than the whole world" and that one drop of Christ's blood would be "sufficient for all the souls of 1000 worlds." *Paradise Lost* has several references to the possibility of other worlds, but Milton is untroubled, except by the practice of all such remote speculation if it diverts prideful man from the true ends of life. And while the religious and scientific Pascal was appalled by the eternal silence of infinite space, for the religious poet — as for the religious and scientific thinker Henry More — there were no terrors in vast space that God fills.

But Milton linked man's fall with the transformation of idyllic Eden into the harsh natural world we know, and that symbolic picture may take us back to a traditional belief which became especially prominent in the late sixteenth and the earlier seventeenth century. It might be called a sort of equivalent of the second law of thermodynamics: nature, including man, had lost its original vitality and was decaying toward its ultimate dissolution. For some time Bacon was almost the sole champion of knowledge and power against the voices of despair. The most voluminous arguments came from two clerics. In *The Fall of Man* (1616) Godfrey Goodman might be said to have combined the themes of Donne's two *Anniversaries*; he stressed the fall and continued sinfulness of man, from which came the corruption of nature, the macrocosm, and he saw no hope except in God's grace and renewed faith. In 1627 George Hakewill, replying to Goodman and the general chorus, saw no evidence of decay except in man's failure of nerve; if roused to resolute activity, he could go forward. The debate is one landmark in the division between pessimists and multiplying progressives. In a short Latin poem the young Milton, as we might expect, repudiated the notion of decay.

A second belief, often connected with the first but less involved with science, was that the world would end six thousand years after its creation; hence, in the early 1600's, man had come more than three fourths of the way through the third and last period of historical time. This idea is perhaps most familiar in one of the richest passages in Donne's sermons (a sermon preached at Whitehall, April 18, 1626), where he uses it in the effort to make conceivable to finite minds the meaning of eternity. The quoting of this is an indulgence, but it will be forgiven.

Qui nec praeceditur hesterno, nec excluditur crastino, A day that hath no *pridie*, nor *post ridie*, yesterday doth not usher it in, nor tomorrow shall not drive it out. Methusalem, with all his hundreds of yeares, was but a Mushrome of a nights growth, to this day, And all the foure Monarchies, with all their thousands of yeares, And all the powerfull Kings, and all the beautifull Queenes of this world, were but as a bed of flowers, some gathered at six, some at seaven, some at eight, All in one Morning, in respect of this Day. In all the two thousand yeares of Nature, before the Law given by Moses, And the two thousand yeares of Law, before the Gospel given by Christ, And the two thousand of Grace, which are running now, (of which last houre we have heard three quarters strike, more then fifteen hundred of this last two thousand spent) In all this six thousand, and in all those, which God may be pleased to adde, *In domo patris*, In this House of his Fathers, there was never heard quarter clock to strike, never seen minute glasse to turne.

Milton, in his last Cambridge oration — a speech, as we noted before, full of Baconian optimism — put what seemed to him defeatist doctrine into the mouth of Ignorance, who would abandon the quest of knowledge because time was now too short to achieve lasting fame. But a generation later Sir Thomas Browne could still affirm that "'Tis too late to be ambitious . . . We whose generations are ordained in this setting part of time, are providentially taken off from such imaginations. . . ." We may observe that, for Donne and Milton and Browne alike, the brevity of earthly time and fame is nothing when weighed against immortality.

These two beliefs or ideas, though they could be involved with science, were themselves hardly scientific, and they invite a reminder of some central and universal facts of life which help more than science to explain some states of the seventeenth-century mind and much of its greatest writing.

The literature of ancient Judea and Greece and Rome, from Job to Juvenal, sets forth, with infinite diversity and power, man's view of the naked human situation and the sickness of civilized society; and our writers were for the most part devoutly Christian heirs of Judea and Greece and Rome and the Middle Ages. Then they had their full share of personal experience, public and private, and their full share of the pessimism always induced by the contrast between what man is and what he might be. To speak only of timeless things, there was the great fact of mutability in individual, national, and world history, which had afflicted pagan and, despite faith in Providence, Hebrew and Christion minds; the weariness and despair of many centuries were concentrated, along with a prayer for the stability of heaven, in the last and most moving stanzas of *The Faerie Queene*. There was the ever-present and personal fact of sin, with all its eternal consequences. To quote George Herbert (*The Agonie*),

> Philosophers have measur'd mountains,
> Fathom'd the depths of seas, of states, and kings,
> Walk'd with a staffe to heav'n, and traced fountains:
> But there are two vast, spacious things,
> The which to measure it doth more behove:
> Yet few there are that sound them; Sinne and Love.

There was, finally, the fact of death, even though it was attended by the trumpet notes of complete faith in immortality. The earlier seventeenth century gave birth to nearly all the greatest meditations on death in English literature — in the King James Bible, Shakespeare, Webster, Donne, Ralegh, Drummond, Bacon, Henry King, Sir Thomas Browne, Jeremy Taylor, Milton, and others. It was not science that evoked these reverberating utterances; the scientific temper would have stifled almost all of them — and did, in the latter part of the century.

One main agent in the process that cooled religion, emotion, and language brings us back to the subject of science from which we have strayed. I mean the tradition of philosophic skepticism which had flourished in antiquity and revived, with increasing scientific support, in the sixteenth and seventeenth centuries. Without trying to define its historical components and variations, one may speak, loosely, of a critical rationalism which took nothing as established and certain and which, in extreme forms, accepted flux and philosophic ignorance and uncertainty as the human condition. Skeptics might start from various positions, abstract skepticism, libertine individualism and naturalism, anti-Christian Deism. Montaigne's question, "What do I know?" was hardly a scientific question, although, as it continued to be asked, it acquired scientific props. Behind it was the growing pressure that came from challenges to authority of all kinds, in the more popular fields of religion and government as well as in science.

It would no doubt be unthinkable to talk about science and seventeenth-century literature without quoting those lines from Donne's *First Anniversary* (1611) which have been quoted a thousand times in the last forty years:

> And new Philosophy calls all in doubt;
> The Element of fire is quite put out;
> The Sun is lost, and th' earth, and no mans wit
> Can well direct him where to looke for it.
> And freely men confesse that this world's spent,
> When in the Planets, and the Firmament
> They seeke so many new; they see that this
> Is crumbled out againe to his Atomies.
> 'Tis all in peeces, all cohaerence gone;
> All just supply, and all Relation.

Some years later William Drummond of Hawthornden echoed Donne in a fuller picture of bewilderment over the discoveries of the new astronomy, and he concluded: "Thus, Sciences by the diverse Motiones of this Globe of the Braine of Man, are become Opiniones, nay, Errores, and leave the Imagination in a thousand Labyrinthes. What is all wee knowe compared with what wee knowe not?"

Donne's lines have often been quoted as proof of "Jacobean pessimism," although the Jacobean age was in the main an optimistic recovery from Elizabethan depression. But our point here is that they have often been quoted as proof that Donne and his fellows were uprooted and confounded by the new science. I have kept this *locus classicus* so long in reserve because it seemed desirable to recall first some of the many other reasons why the seventeenth century was, as every age is for men of imaginative intelligence, an age of anxiety. Donne felt those general pressures; also, he was writing after years of heavy personal trials. But he was not a scientific modernist in the Baconian sense; still less was he a skeptical modern intellectual lost in a meaningless universe. So far as we know, Donne never at any time in his life entertained doubts of the Christian faith. In the two *Anniversaries* his purpose was self-analysis, a spiritual stocktaking, and — like Godfrey Goodman a little later, as we observed — he pictured nature's decay and man's sinful intellectual pride, ignorance, and confusion in contrast with the one sure resource, religion; hence he freely used new science, old science, and fable, as these served his turn at the moment. So, too, William Drummond's melancholy reflections issued in an ecstatic vision of the soul returning to its heavenly home. One could not readily name any man of the seventeenth century whose religious belief was overthrown by science, as it so often was in the nineteenth — though in the latter part of the century we do find the natural theology of Deism emerging as a main current.

One kind of reaction to the rapid growth of knowledge, especially but not merely science, was so common in the earlier part of the period that we must take note of it: that is, the fear of excessive "curiosity," of knowledge outrunning wisdom and faith, of the quest of secular knowledge and power that led to the pride and the fall of Adam and Eve. For a cloud of witnesses I may refer to Howard Schultz's *Milton and Forbidden Knowledge*; here I can mention only four—I quote laymen partly because they were poets and partly because some later bishops were buoyant Baconians. Among the most moving pictures of intellectual and moral disorder and most urgent pleas for wisdom were those of the Christian-Stoic George Chapman and the darkly Calvinistic statesman Fulke Greville. Then, as a pendant to the lines from Donne's *First Anniversary*, we may recall the long passage in the *Second* where he catalogues examples of the ignorance that attends new scientific discoveries and speculations, here mainly concerning human physiology; and Donne ends, like Robert Burton and others, by leaving the ultimate revelation to faith and heaven.

Our last witness, Milton, had in his youth felt no qualms in celebrating the Baconian conquest of nature, but in *Paradise Lost* Eve is seduced by Satan's specious temptation of godlike knowledge and power beyond human limits. This theme, which is central in the poem—and which is partly developed in the dialogue on astronomy—is re-emphasized in the conclusion. After the penitent Adam has declared his newly and hardly won ideal of Christian faith, humility, obedience, and love, the archangel replies, in lines akin to those quoted a while ago from George Herbert:

> This having learnt, thou hast attaind the Summe
> Of wisdome; hope no higher, though all the Starrs
> Thou knewst by name, and all th' ethereal Powers,
> All secrets of the deep, all Natures works,
> Or works of God in Heav'n, Aire, Earth, or Sea. . . .

And Adam, leaving Paradise for the grim world of history, has before him the hope, not of membership in the Royal Society, but of achieving a happier paradise within himself.

Looking about our own world, which reaches toward the angels chiefly through rockets and missiles, we can hardly say that the many seventeenth-century men who set wisdom above knowledge and power were obscurantists. And that they were not attacking men of straw we realize when we consider the intellectual and moral climate of the Restoration period, the effects of the first modern scientific philosophies. We must take for granted the discoveries of science proper, such as the law of inertia, an approach to modern atomism, and the mathematical workings of gravity, which, to use Dryden's words again, revealed almost a new Nature.

On its highest level, critical rationalism was represented by the expert mathematician Descartes, whose philosophy left room for God and mind, and the would-be mathematician Hobbes, who left room for neither (at least in recognizable form). In England Descartes was, at least for a time, loudly applauded, while Hobbes was the great bogeyman of a whole generation of conservatives. Yet the doctrine or main drift of Descartes was hardly less destructive of traditional values, religious, ethical, and imaginative, than the thoroughgoing mechanistic materialism of Hobbes; and Descartes seems to have had even less historical and cultural sensibility than Hobbes (who began with a translation of Thucydides and ended with a verse translation of Homer). In brief, the acid of critical rationalism, sprayed over the whole field of intellect and imagination, exterminated, slowly, many tares and cockles which had long flourished in the human mind and obscured its vision of truth; and it destroyed, in time, such poisonous weeds as belief in witchcraft. But it also ate at the roots of religious and imaginative belief, of myth and symbol, by which the age, like earlier ages, had lived. The traditional world view could not easily be translated into the terms of mass and velocity, mechanism and atomism. God the Father and Creator became the first cause of motion, a ghostly *x*. Man, the lord of creation, became a superfluous accident outside the cosmic machine. The human mind was still a microcosm, but not in the old sense; it was now a miniature system of bodies in motion. The will, the moral rudder of man's ship, became the last, decisive appetite in a deterministic sequence. The great chain of being dwindled from a dynamic vision to a Deistic formula. Nature, "the Art of God," might still support the "argument from design," but the treasury of emblems and divine hieroglyphics and "signatures" became for progressive scientists a system of forces to be measured and exploited. The network of analogies and correspondences which had made all creation a living unity dissolved in the cold dry light of fact and reason. The music of the spheres was no longer audible to the spiritual ear; and the phoenix remained dead in its ashes. Even if parts of this revolution took place chiefly in the mind of Hobbes, the climate was greatly changed. We might try to imagine Donne's picture of eternity in a sermon of Tillotson's, or the conclusion of *Urn-Burial* or *The Garden of Cyrus* in Locke's *Essay concerning Human Understanding*. The Adam of Dryden's operatic version of *Paradise Lost* appeals to Hobbesian determinism.

We cannot, however, overlook the later Cambridge Platonists, Henry More and Ralph Cudworth, who, accepting the new science, strove to reinterpret and reassert traditional views and values against Descartes and Hobbes. More's account of God and space influenced Newton; his insistence on the reality of spirit, on the unity of the world, was to come to life again in Coleridge and Wordsworth, and supported Yeats when he recoiled from the "grey truth" of science. We might, too, think of such an ally of More and Cudworth as the eminent naturalist, John Ray; and of a work of grandiose "scientific" imagination by a student of More and Cudworth, Thomas Burnet's *Sacred Theory of the Earth*, which might be called a kind of geological *Paradise Lost* or a sequel to both the pessimistic Godfrey Goodman and the optimistic George Hakewill, and which started a tidal wave of controversy. Then, too, though his meditations in prose and verse were not published, there was Traherne's religious response to ideas of infinity.

But these men did not set or represent the tone of Restoration literature. In the new world the soul did not experience its old visions and agonies, nor was language available to express them. There is a gulf between Donne's contrasting of the Church Universal of Scripture and the divided church of history—

Show me deare Christ, thy spouse, so bright and cleare . . .

and Dryden's earnest desire for an absolute authority:

Such an Omniscient Church we wish indeed;
'Twere worth Both Testaments, and cast in the Creed.

And we might add, though such parallels are quite unfair to Dryden's genius, two pictures of the resurrection:

At the round earths imagin'd corners, blow
Your trumpets, Angells, and arise, arise
From death, you numberlesse infinities
Of soules, and to your scattred bodies goe . . .

When ratling Bones together fly
From the four Corners of the Skie . . .

The new poetic temper was adumbrated by Sir William Davenant and Hobbes in their discussion of Davenant's *Gondibert* (1650). The kind of heroic poetry now acceptable was the rational depiction of "nature," of mundane actuality, freed from the supernatural fictions of traditional epic and romance. The stage was set for Restoration comedy and the political satires of Dryden and others — including Marvell, who in a more propitious age had been a uniquely complex, subtle, and sensitive metaphysical lyrist. In general, to repeat the commonest of commonplaces, Restoration literature is rational, civilized, public; it shuns "Enthusiasm" and knows no mysteries.

In the civilizing process, science and scientific rationalism played both negative and positive roles. We might think of Isaac Barrow's and Newton's view of poetry as "a kind of ingenious nonsense," or of Locke's virtually similar opinion. But a more useful witness is Thomas Sprat, in his *History of the Royal Society*. Sprat did not oppose all poetry (indeed his own bad poems won him the name of "Pindaric Sprat"), and the future bishop did not reject the Bible as a poetic quarry, but his great hope for poetry was in a nature purged of fable and consonant with scientific truth. This was no doubt an inevitable aim, yet it typifies the division the age was making between the old and the modern world and the death of the unified and "magical" and fundamentally religious vision which had given birth to so much great writing. At any rate scientific discovery and thought continued on their triumphant course. Science was being so far assimilated and accommodated as to provide a new basis of intellectual security; and Newton's conceptions of the nature of light and the cosmic order came to inspire new raptures of illuminated understanding, if seldom good poetry. This sense of security may be said to be reflected in the march of the now dominant heroic couplet, in contrast with the infinite variety of earlier lyrical and private verse.

As for the technique of prose, we identify the earlier part of the century (some of whose writers survived into the newer world) with the richly figurative eloquence of Donne, Milton, Browne, and Jeremy Taylor. In that earlier period plain prose had been written in far greater abundance, in histories, pamphlets, textbooks, and many other forms, but, in general, plain diction did not make the kind of modern prose established by Dryden, disciplined syntax and symmetry as well as urbane conversational ease. There were various causes for the change, among them the anti-Ciceronian movement in which Bacon had been a leader. But it is the Baconian scientific ideal that concerns us. The bare precision of Hobbes was one early portent of the new philosophic and scientific prose. The general diffusion of the rational and scientific temper affected all kinds of writing, even the sermon, and Jeremy Taylor's poetic flights were frowned upon by Restoration divines. One scientific bishop attacked both the Cambridge Platonists and "enthusiastic" sectaries for cloudy, figurative language, and wished for "an Act of Parliament to abridge Preachers the use of fulsom and lushious Metaphors." In science the spearhead of the movement was the Royal Society. The one famous passage in Sprat's *History* is his proclamation of the ideal of exact, denotative language as the necessary medium of scientific knowledge and thought.

However necessary that was, the general climate, as we have seen, affected nonscientific prose, and it could not but affect poetry too. Whereas Shakespeare and his fellows had thought in metaphors, the most complexly expressive mode of thought and feeling, the main texture of Restoration verse was prose statement, more explicit and denotative than figurative. At the same time, science as well as neoclassical theory contributed to a kind of abstractionism which had begun to appear long before, that is, a partial shift from concrete particulars to generalized concepts, the phrases that go under the name of Augustan "poetic diction."

The literally epoch-making changes in outlook and expression that have been sketchily summarized belonged no doubt to the inevitable process of growing up, the making of the modern mind. Happily the process remains incomplete, since the poetic vision has not yet been killed by the spirit of positivism, though many modern poets have been consciously oppressed by the withering of "myth" in a scientific and technological civilization. Looking back at the seventeenth century, we can hardly deny that for literature progress entailed far greater losses than gains, that one large effect of science was to circumscribe, blunt, and impoverish the rich, all-embracing sensibility and expressive power that had flourished in the earlier period. The writers of poetry and prose whom we chiefly read and reread are the great race who lived before or outside the Enlightenment.

The Humanities

Because "the humanities" comprise such diverse media, methods, and aims, and because I am not a universal doctor, I shall use literature as most central and representative. I shall try to deal with three main topics: the humanistic tradition of the past, its modern equivalents in scholarship, criticism, and teaching, and the general character and objects of literary study; the cultural climate outside as well as inside the university and its effect on the status and claims of the humanities, especially the powerful attractions and pressures of the modern scientific and technological revolution; and, by way of final summary, the universal, unique, and irreplaceable role of the humanities in expressing and providing experience and discipline that are both aesthetic and ethical, the communication of an individual vision of life to other individuals. If these headings are or invite clichés, an inhabitant of our world may believe that they are in continual need of being reaffirmed. The need is urgent at a time when scientists and psychologists tell us that, thanks to scientific control of our environment and to the cure of human weaknesses by appropriate drugs, there is less and less occasion for intellectual and moral struggle.[1]

Reprinted by permission from *Daedalus* (published by the American Academy of Arts and Sciences, Brookline, Massachusetts), vol. 93, no. 4, "The Contemporary University: U.S.A." (Fall 1964).

[1] Robert S. Morison, *Daedalus*, Fall 1964, p. 1136; B. F. Skinner, *Proceedings of the American Philosophical Society*, CVIII (1964),

The ultimate goal of some advanced thinkers appears to be a race of moral robots manipulated by social engineers.

Since the essential aim of humanistic studies remains what it always has been, we might look briefly at the historical pattern. To go no further back than to the Renaissance humanists, who so ardently revived and molded the Greco-Roman tradition, *studia humanitatis* and similar terms comprised classical literature, history, and philosophy; these were the chief studies worthy of a free man, the kinds of liberal knowledge that nourished *homo sapiens*, that is, man as man, a human and social personality, not as a professional or technical expert. There was no modern division into humanities, social sciences, and natural sciences, since the classical writings comprised all three (and one great strength of classical education has been just that). If the early humanists, like Erasmus, were mainly indifferent to science (which had not yet become conspicuously important), some, from Rabelais to Milton, were not. But the central ideal of serious European humanists embraced intellectual cultivation and taste, rational and moral discipline, and civic responsibility — qualities which had been united in the great exemplar, Cicero, a moral teacher and magistrate as well as a model of style. The humanists looked backward in order to look forward; the classics mirrored a civilization that must be re-created as a basis for further progress toward the good life.

But the good life now included Christian faith, and many of the leading humanists, Italian as well as northern, were earnest Christians. They saw the humanities as comple-

482–85. For a humanistic philosopher's comment on the behaviorist symposium that occupied this issue of the *Proceedings*, see Brand Blanshard, ibid., CIX (1965), 22–28.

mentary, not antagonistic, to Christianity and they carried on in more practical terms the medieval philosophic synthesis; as Cicero had said, *sapientia* is the knowledge of things human and divine. The noblest pagans had, by the light of natural reason, approached Christian ethics and faith, and the traditional alliance was unforgettably registered in Erasmus' echo of the liturgy, *Sancte Socrates, ora pro nobis*. One basic part of the synthesis was the conception of man as midway between the beasts and the angels and pulled by his animal and angelic impulses in opposed directions. If to the modern mind that idea seems quaint, it was, as an ethical and religious concept, a main source of the strength, health, and centrality of Renaissance literature, from Shakespeare down.

The primary humanistic activity was the editing, translating, interpreting, and teaching of the classics, and many men went on to application and emulation, to the writing of literature, history, and philosophy, especially for the guidance of rulers, and some were themselves engaged in public affairs. Though the division of labor was beginning, few were confined to one groove. Outside of humanism proper, the versatility of Renaissance artists has long been a byword. Within the ranks, to mention a name or two, the bold philologist Lorenzo Valla wrote on ethics and on the New Testament and used philology to show that the Donation of Constantine, the document that had buttressed papal claims to temporal power, was a late forgery. Juan Luis Vives, along with writing books on classical-Christian education, was a pioneer in psychology and sociology. Copernicus got clues from ancient astronomers. But the cardinal fact is that for centuries Europe had a cultural solidarity that transcended national and religious boundaries. Indeed one object of such men as Erasmus was the abolition of war and the creation of international peace; that special effort of course failed, but Erasmus, the Christian humanist *par excellence*, had more effect on the European mind than any other writer between St. Augustine and Voltaire. All or almost all the great original thinkers and writers had more or less of the same kind of classical education and read, spoke, and wrote the same language, literally or metaphorically or both — Copernicus, Kepler, and Galileo, Machiavelli, Ariosto, and Tasso, Calvin, Rabelais, and Montaigne, Erasmus, Sir Thomas More, Spenser, Shakespeare, Bacon, Milton, and a host of others. In fact, down through a good part of the nineteenth century most of the great men of Europe and America were brought up on the classics; their modern counterparts in wisdom and style are not so numerous as increases in population and enlightenment might lead us to expect.

Today, in our very different world, the natural and the social sciences are of course separate realms. The humanities have lost history to the social sciences (though some historians maintain their allegiance to Clio), and have gained music and the fine arts. Philosophy is still counted as one of the humanities although the nature of most modern philosophy would seem to place it with mathematics and science. Humanists may regard divinity as an ally or an alien. Literature, as the most direct and comprehensive expression of human concerns and the most generally accessible body of material, remains central. Along with such internal changes there is a large fact that complicates discussion: that practitioners of the humanities fall into two different groups — scholars, critics, and teachers on the one side and creative artists on the other — a much more distinct cleavage, in spite of mainly common interests, than the mere difference in intellectual power between scientific explorers and scientific teachers. In this connection we may notice a recent phenomenon most conspicuous in the United States, the inviting of creative artists for prolonged visits or lifetime posts in colleges and universities. Josiah Royce observed long ago that a philosopher was expected to spiritualize the community; but now that the philosopher often limits himself to semanticizing the community, that function has fallen to the humanist, and the artist — who may or may not be scholarly — is introduced to help spiritualize the academy as well as the community. Such minds may bring provocative, unacademic freshness to the teaching of their art, and their presence is a reminder that literature, for instance, is not something always embalmed in fat anthologies but written by people who live among us and pay taxes.

Since no one, even if much more learned than I, could discuss all branches of the humanities in a few — or in many — pages, and since literature is, as I said, the most central and has the largest professional following, I shall stick mainly to it. Here a great and obvious change from the many earlier centuries must be registered at the start: that in the English-speaking world the ancient classics have been almost wholly replaced by English. The academic study of English has been a fairly recent thing; it used to be assumed that no one needed instruction in his own language and literature. Whatever the faults of traditional classical teaching (and they were often grievous), the great change — however inevitable in our changed world — has brought loss as well as gain. For one thing, it has not improved the English spoken and written by the educated; "the new illiteracy" is evident everywhere. On another level, there has been and can be no adequate substitute for authentic and active contact with the classical tradition, which has always been both a revolutionary and a steadying force.

Before we consider various modern approaches to literature it may be said that that word is not restricted to the purely imaginative, that it retains its humanistic breadth of meaning. Indeed the imaginative part of literature is perhaps smaller in bulk than the heterogeneous mass of prose, ancient and modern, which also comes under that head. Here the modern barriers that divide the humanities, the natural sciences, and the social sciences simply disappear, because works in all these areas may or must be accepted as humanistic classics if they fulfill certain conditions: they must appeal to *homo sapiens*, the general reader; that appeal must endure from age to age; and there must be special distinction of substance, form, and style — art, in short — even if the author's purpose was quite utilitarian. If such conditions sound vague, there is not much doubt in concrete cases, when time has done its sifting. But we are concerned here with imaginative writing, since that is what distinguishes literature from all other forms of thought and expression.

The study of literature has itself many areas and levels and consequently many diverse specialists. Some kinds of work carry on what was begun in antiquity and revived during the Renaissance, though their scope is now widely extended. There are many biographical and bibliographical tasks, the determination of authorship, of dates of composition, and so on. One prerequisite for serious study is the establishment of authentic texts, not merely of old writers like Shakespeare but of such moderns as Poe, Hawthorne, and Whitman. Of late years, it may be observed, the labor of collating texts has been much eased and accelerated by ingenious machines; and machines have likewise transformed the making of such useful tools as concordances. But one can only begin to suggest the variety and refinements of such primary tasks of scholarship; in themselves these may be less humanistic than scientific, though their ultimate object is not.

That ultimate object, as we all know, is to understand and interpret works of literature in their full aesthetic and substantive significance and to make them available to readers, to preserve and transmit our great heritage as a living possession. Whereas science means only the latest knowledge (unless scientists cultivate scientific history as a personal interest), great works of art are never dead or superseded; they remain not only alive but unique. The body of literature from Homer and the Bible to the present is, in the fullest humanistic sense, a timeless whole. On the other hand, the literature of Europe — not to mention the literatures of Asia and America, Australasia and Africa — comprises that of many countries, and this vast body of writing reflects the civilization, the beliefs, ideas, and manners, the language and literary modes, of many times and places; and, though the very definition of a classic is that it transcends time and place, these facts of remoteness are initial barriers. The past, or rather a great many pasts, must be re-created, since, however relevant works of art may be to us in our time, they must first be understood on their own terms, as products of particular minds in particular settings. Indeed, as Lionel Trilling has emphasized, their very pastness is a part of their meaning for us. Unless we are willing to miss or misread a great deal, we have to use bifocal lenses; and such lenses mean every resource we can muster in the way of information, imagination, and disciplined intelligence.

During the several generations since professional literary

scholarship began in the United States, there have been successive waves of distinct character. (Criticism in the nineteenth and the early twentieth century was largely of the impressionistic kind represented by Poe and Lowell and many others.) The first — and for a long time virtually the sole — scholarly method was derived from both the science and the literary theory of Europe and might be labeled genetic: this was the writing of literary history in terms of sources and influences, and such things were mostly clearly traceable in medieval and postmedieval literature. This prolonged effort accomplished much by discovering and ordering a mass of solidly factual data, but such literary history, though necessary and valuable, was more or less external and it led to revolt. The next phase, which began before 1920, was the history of ideas: religious, philosophical, ethical, social, political, scientific, aesthetic ideas. The history of literature was rewritten at a new depth, and such cultural history became an important discipline in itself; it has been still more important in enriching our comprehension of countless individual works.

But the history of ideas, like the older literary history, did not in itself carry any criteria of aesthetic value, since a mediocre author may illustrate ideologies or influences no less or better than a great one. And here the so-called "new criticism" stepped into the partial vacuum to concentrate on interpretation and evaluation of the individual work — usually though not always a short poem. This movement has done much to right the balance and keep the prime object of study before us, and it has greatly quickened insight into subtleties of texture, imagery, and tone. It has also revealed its limitations and, like the earlier approaches, it can be inadequate by itself. While these several methods have continued in operation, others have developed during the past forty years, especially through the impact of psychology and anthropology. What may be loosely termed the Freudian line needs no explanation — though its tendency to rely on formulas often needs correction. What may be loosely termed the Jungian line has been concerned with the working of archetypal myths upon the creative imagination and with the poetic language of symbols. The latest arrivals have been the structural linguists, who seem to promise much new light, though I confess that I have not encountered it — or perhaps have not sought it with proper zeal. Some other schools of thought, from the sociological to the neo-Aristotelian, must be passed by. These various approaches, or some of them, have stimulated fresh and more or less valuable kinds of perception; they have also yielded irresponsible fancies unchecked by historical knowledge and understanding.

This brief survey covers what has happened in English (including American studies since their rapid expansion began). Nowadays graduate teachers may not be omniscient sages, and graduate students are often deficient in breadth of reading, in writing, and in foreign languages, but the requirements and aims of graduate study have changed enormously for the better. Bibliographical training, of the kind touched on above, is available for those who want it, but it is an instrument, not an end in itself. Graduate students, as eager human beings and as prospective teachers, are in graduate courses concerned entirely or almost entirely with the fundamentals of literature and ideas, with aesthetic and philosophic criticism based on substantial historical knowledge. This is a world away from the mainly dusty grind that older generations went through decades ago. Whatever the deep personal devotion to literature of the illustrious scholars of those days, the mystique of graduate study seemed to start from the assumption that mature students left behind them not only hope but any humanistic concern with man, life, and the meaning of literature (I speak of the tracts of desert, not of the oases). The titles of doctoral theses now written all over the country bear concrete testimony to the great predominance of interpretative, philosophical, and aesthetic criticism. What worries graduate teachers nowadays, along with a frequent consciousness of their own shortcomings, is the frequent inadequacy of preparation and capacity in graduate students, the several kinds of deficiency mentioned above.

Today, moreover, undergraduate courses, graduate courses and seminars, and a large proportion of the books and articles written by college and university teachers are all of a piece, a coherent progression in depth. Learning and criticism are not divorced as they used to be. The various approaches to literature which I outlined are all in simultaneous operation in literary departments. In going on with an account of the humanities, therefore, I see no reason to consider "research" by the most mature scholar-critics as something remotely and austerely different from what is done in undergraduate courses. The planets are all revolving at various distances from the same sun and receive varying portions of the same light, sometimes a bit refracted.

Whatever weaknesses or excesses there have been (and the natural and social sciences have their share of these), the total accomplishment of modern scholarship and criticism has been immense. If we cannot claim such revolutionary advances as science has made, we can say that at the present time the vast and varied literature of the past is far better understood in all its aspects than it ever was before. In the nature of the case there can be no final interpretation of the more complex works of art; as the history of Shakespearian criticism makes amply clear, some ages see and emphasize some elements, other ages other elements. Still, with all the cross-currents and eddies and occasional waterfalls, there is a general movement along or toward a central channel; as Shakespeare's name again makes clear, peripheral fluctuations do not affect the stability of the general pattern. One cause for misgiving is that this modern enlightenment — and the active interest in literature of the past that kindles the enlightenment — is so largely academic. Criticism in general, in reaching new subtleties of insight, has become a specialized esoteric preserve; there are very few American critics who can be said to address and be heard by the educated community in something like the fashion of Arnold or Sainte-Beuve. But the educated public does not seem to care much about criticism of any kind; if a biography of a literary figure tries to smuggle in critical or philosophical ideas, popular reviewers brand it as highbrow and heavy.

The most cursory survey of scholarly criticism is a needless reminder that, on the higher levels, it grows out of individual knowledge, reflection, and intuition. It cannot, any more than creation, be the result of teamwork. It is obvious also that important criticism is the product of maturity, that it must grow out of experience of life and wisdom as well as out of intellectual knowledge. A commonplace fact of scientific history is that many scientists have made their chief contributions at a very early age; for the humanist a corresponding accomplishment would be next to impossible. Also, whereas under similar conditions two or more scientists may independently and simultaneously arrive at a similar idea (like Darwin and Wallace), no two artists would produce anything like similar works of art, since the scientific discovery is not a distinctively personal vision and the work of art is. And of course "discovery" is not the aim of humanistic study. There is discovery of a kind, to be sure, and reinterpretation is continually going on, but the humanist's great aim is the achieving and sharing of the experience given by works of art. And the all-important thing about that is that the experience is an individual affair. Whatever insights may be held in common, no one person can respond in exactly the same way as any other person. When a scientist has a boldly imaginative idea, that idea is made completely and uniformly intelligible to other scientists; but the intuitions of a humanist are not fully demonstrable and cannot be transferred *in toto* to other minds — as indeed the original work of art may not have completely rendered its author's conception or yielded its full import to the best of critics. The inevitable degree of imprecision in the study of literature and the other arts may to the rigorous scientific reason count as a defect in the humanities; but most of the really important things in life cannot be measured.

The ultimate and obvious aims of literary study have already been indicated, but they may be put in ampler terms, though still with pragmatic simplicity. The raw human animal, more acquisitive, aggressive, and sensual than sensitive, needs to be civilized if society and the good life are to exist. The humanities are in their very nature the chief agents of the civilizing process, since they are the distillation of universal human experience. Through the senses, the imagination (both immediate and historical), the affections, and the critical intelligence literature and the other arts enlarge and enrich the individual's very limited experience and refine and discipline his sensibility and mind and character; and there are no other agents that perform these functions on both aesthetic and ethical planes (not that we read works of art for therapeutic reasons but that full enjoyment and assimilation have therapeutic results). We might think, for instance, of what a world is added to our imaginative and moral consciousness by *Hamlet* or *King Lear*. Moreover, since traditional religion has so largely lost its power, many people, young and old, find through the humanities their chief or only understanding of man's religious quest. The greatest works of artistic creation — and the greatest are essentially religious — provide a vision of reality that nothing else provides. Of course —as I have remarked elsewhere—it cannot be demonstrated with graphs that John or Betty Smith, through responding to a work of art, became a person of richer imaginative and moral insight, of finer taste and wisdom and stability; but throughout all generations that has been an experience for some people. If it had not been, our individual and communal lives would be solitary, poor, nasty, brutish, and short.

It may be asked why, if the humanities do all this, our world is what it is, why we are not living in a utopia of peace and culture. To repeat an answer I once gave (an answer that drew a gibe from a sociologist), the humanities have always had to contend with nothing less universal and inveterate than original sin. This comprehensive generality may be translated into more specific terms because the standing of the humanities within the university is strongly affected by the cultural climate outside. Public indifference to the humanities has always existed, even in ancient Athens and Renaissance Europe, and Gresham's law operates in the cultural as well as in the monetary sphere. In our country, in spite of occasional splashes of publicity about the newsworthy aspects of the fine arts and the performing arts, the mass of the educated public seem to have relatively little interest in literature of the past. The sale of paperbacks is a not altogether reliable index to the amount of private reading done outside of college courses, and the interest of college students often seems to end with their last examination. While the humanities, creative or critical, require mainly the time and effort of individuals and not the huge sums that go into scientific research, their unique and fundamental value does need public understanding, respect, and support. A few people, including some scientists and even members of Congress, have urged active recognition, and the newly established Commission on the Humanities and a possible National Humanities Foundation may do something to awaken proper concern.

In addition to the philistinism that thrives everywhere, a special strain runs through the American tradition. (Some of the founding fathers were cultivated intellectuals, but nowadays they might not be elected to public office.) Puritanism (which had its intellectuals but had begun its anti-humanistic campaign in England), egalitarian democracy, the spirit of the frontier, belief in practical utility, and the conviction that the business of America is business have fostered distrust or dislike of "culture," of any use of the mind for intangible ends, of being different from the crowd. Only in the last few years — and because of the Sputnik, not for intellectual reasons — has there been any general revolt against the pedagogical doctrine and practice that have dominated the schools in our century: "adjustment to life" instead of education and, among other things, the conception of literature as an attractive appendage to social studies.[2] One need not cite the familiar evidence of popular taste supplied by the mass media (which are not peculiar to the United States).

If the relative lack of zeal for the humanities among us is to be attributed to the nature of our society, one large heading under that vague phrase is the many-sided pressure of science. The dazzling achievements, the prestige, the practical value, and the high rewards of scientific and technological research are more than obvious. For decades the philanthropic foundations poured out oceans of aid for the natural and social sciences and a trickle for the humanities (of late years there has been a turn for the better). Government money flows into university laboratories for research in military technology. Reaching the moon seems to be more urgent than our many social and educational needs. Every spring and summer, when college graduates enter the job market, students of the humanities are at or near the foot of the salary scale, scientists of course at the top;[3] and, while philosophic captains of industry tell Commencement throngs of the prime need for humanely educated men, their personnel officers are hiring technical experts.[4] The undergraduate as well as the graduate study of science appears to be almost wholly professional[5] and leads directly to high pay and security,

[2] On the study of literature one must cite the devastating survey by James J. Lynch and Bertrand Evans, *High School English Textbooks: A Critical Examination* (Boston, 1963).

[3] A summary report by Fred M. Hechinger, *New York Times*, June 9, 1963.

[4] Richard Schlatter, *University* (Princeton), no. 10 (Fall 1961).

[5] Ernest Nagel, "The Place of Science in a Liberal Education," *Daedalus*, Winter 1959, p. 63. Gerald Holton has pleaded for more and better courses in science for nonscientific students in "Science for Nonscientists," *Teachers College Record*, LXIV (1963), 497–508.

while the humanities are, by mundane reckoning, quite useless.

Since the functions of the humanities were earlier summed up in simple terms, I may say briefly what I understand to be the functions of the sciences. The investigation of the terrestrial and cosmic world and the human body and mind is an essential and noble fulfillment of man's quest for knowledge; the discovery and interpretation of scientific knowledge grow out of methods that are an essential part of a liberal education; and the uses to which such knowledge has been put have enormously affected every individual by improving the conditions of life in an infinite variety of ways. This we all know and believe. The social sciences may be described in corresponding terms: their material is the social, economic, and behavioral patterns of mankind in the mass. But to say that the natural and social sciences and the humanities all look toward the benefit of man is to obscure the basic differences among these disciplines and to allow the implication that imbalance does not matter much, or that the sciences, with all their glamor of modernity, have superseded the humanities and should now take over the guidance of mankind. The last implication is a matter of course for a number of people, for example, Derek J. Price, the historian of science: "Now that science has become the chief determinant of world civilization . . ." [6]

The academic role of the humanities cannot be understood or assessed without reference to both the rightful role of science and the claims sometimes made for it as the supreme oracle of modern man. Of course some scientists and social scientists are earnest and vocal supporters

[6] *Teachers College Record*, LXIV (1963), 531. Some representatives of various attitudes are cited in my next few paragraphs.

of the humanities, but there is in the air enough extravagant one-sidedness to be disturbing. To quote a casual but suggestive utterance, an eminent social scientist probably spoke for more than himself when he said to me, "I suppose poetry nowadays is on the way out." One gets the impression that humanists — the special custodians of all the great literature and art that man has produced — can now be seen as laggards behind the triumphal march, as forlorn attendants in an empty museum.

This general attitude has been recurrent ever since Bacon and Descartes excluded poetry from the world of scientific reality. I should like to cite a few heterogeneous writers on science, as representative both of scientific thought and of notions of the humanities and science that one meets in various areas and on various levels. For F. S. C. Northrop[7] modern science is the infallible lawgiver in all things, and not merely Dante (his example) but all literature that makes serious use of beliefs and ideas not now scientifically valid is dead at its center. There can be no values except those determined by science; people's emotions have long been attached to mistaken ideas and scientific reason must correct these fatal vagaries. "Without the *Weltanschauung* of modern science," says a later writer, in *Science*, "no form of thinking, feeling, or reacting has validity today." [8] Even in our ultrascientific world are any of us, scientists or humanists, moved by scientific principles when we examine ourselves (if we do), when we fall in love or face a moral dilemma, when we feel, think, and act as citizen, friend, son, brother, husband, father — in all the situations in which man lives as man and becomes the subject of literature? To quote a historian

[7] *The Logic of the Sciences and the Humanities* (New York, 1947).
[8] Joseph Gallant, *Science*, CXXV (1957), 787–91.

of science (who cites Henri Poincaré to the same effect):

> For neither in public nor in private life can science establish an ethic. It tells what we can do, never what we should. Its absolute incompetence in the realm of values is a necessary consequence of the objective posture.[9]

In regard to science and the nature of man one central kind of opposition is between optimists and pessimists. On the one hand, some look forward with high confidence to endless progress through endless extension of scientific knowledge. In spite of our oceans of ignorance, said Dr. Conant, "we can set no limits to the future expansion of the 'empire of the mind.'"[10] "No one," says Philippe Le Corbeiller, "can set limits to what science might achieve."[11] But other prophets of science tell us, with a sort of sadistic relish — one cannot say masochistic because they themselves are apparently outside the human race — that men are only lumps of impure carbon and water, links in a deterministic chain, nodes in a communication network. The first of these definitions of man is Lord Russell's old phrase; the third was used at a *Daedalus* conference in May 1963, without, so far as I recall, any protest except from my unreconstructed self. If a man is only a node in a communication network he obviously cannot be a scientist, much less can he ordain human values and destiny — though it would appear that his mental wiring can encounter a short circuit. We might remember that Adolf

[9] C. C. Gillispie, *The Edge of Objectivity* (Princeton, 1960) p. 154. For similar views, cf. the scientist Bentley Glass, *Science and Liberal Education* (Baton Rouge, 1959), pp. 84–85, and the humanist Moody E. Prior, *Science and the Humanities* (Evanston, 1962), pp. 17–18, etc.

[10] *Modern Science and Modern Man* (New York, 1952), p. 111.

[11] *Daedalus*, Winter 1959, p. 171. I make special use of this issue because its subject, "Education in the Age of Science," is highly relevant and because such a symposium is handy for readers of *Daedalus*.

Eichmann, examined by half a dozen psychiatrists, was pronounced, according to the best scientific standards, completely normal; and he was a completely efficient node. A humanist would be happier with the high than with the low view of man, though he would like some qualifications and additions.

Lord Snow's main object, humanitarian action on behalf of the hordes of people living in subhuman conditions, was more central in his second discourse[12] than in his first. But we remember his strange assertion that the second law of thermodynamics is about the scientific equivalent of a work of Shakespeare — as if the two were comparable except on the level of mere data of knowledge. A philosophic scientist, Dean Robert B. Lindsay, in *The Role of Science in Civilization* (1963), takes a broadly receptive view of the humanities, but even he can be myopic on a central point. Arguing (pp. 44f) that science includes value judgments, he says that decisions have to be made among opposed scientific theories. But these are not value judgments at all, unless the term is stretched out of recognition. They cannot be value judgments unless the constituents of atoms and cells are moral agents whose motives and behavior are being scrutinized on moral grounds. This is the very *sine qua non* of literature, and Dean Lindsay is not the only scientist who misses the point. (What some behavioral scientists would say one need not inquire.) It is often said — by Dean Lindsay and others — that scientists must be grouped with artists because both use imagination to interpret data, but such a statement merely befogs the issue. The kind of imagination that interprets the nonmoral secrets of the atom or the cell

[12] "The Two Cultures: A Second Look," *Times Literary Supplement*, October 25, 1963.

is completely different from the ethical imagination that explores the workings of human nature.

Two other witnesses, on opposite sides of the fence, may be mentioned. The late Aldous Huxley in his *Literature and Science* (1963) took a line that was very odd for the author of *Brave New World* (1932). He made a tour among the sciences in order to show the kinds of new knowledge the modern writer must assimilate and learn to use. Recalling what the nightingale's song had meant to Keats and Arnold and Eliot, he explained that the bird sings to warn other birds that it is staking out its time and territory for the consumption of caterpillars. This was not, as one might think, a spoof, but a scientific exposure of poetic fallacy — and totally irrelevant. On the other hand, Dean Barzun, in his *Science: The Glorious Entertainment* (1964), pictured modern man and civilization as thoroughly deranged by science and technology and the climate they have created. While the picture may be overdrawn, some reactions from the scientific establishment seemed to imply that the noted author was a brash schoolboy making faces at the teacher; the book shows, said one reviewer, what scientists are up against in presenting their case to the world (*New York Times Book Review*, April 5, 1964).

For a last witness on this general point we might hear a scientist of broad horizons, Loren Eiseley:

> Even now in the enthusiasm for new discoveries, reported public interviews with scientists tend to run increasingly toward a future replete with more inventions, stores of energy, babies in bottles, deadlier weapons. Relatively few have spoken of values, ethics, art, religion — all those intangible aspects of life which set the tone of a civilization and determine, in the end, whether it will be cruel or humane; whether, in other words, the modern world, so far as its

interior spiritual life is concerned, will be stainless steel like its exterior, or display the rich fabric of genuine human experience. The very indifference of many scientists to such matters reveals how far man has already gone toward the world of the "outside," of no memory, of contempt toward all that makes up the human tradition.[13]

One might also quote Margaret Mead's remark — made in a different context — that nowadays "students of the humanities, as they lost their hold on contemporary developments in science, began to stress their monopoly of eternal values." [14] Miss Mead perhaps overlooked our long-lived contemporary, Plato.

The fundamental differences between science and the humanities are not at all the same thing as differences between scientists and humanists, but something may be said about the latter, since the questions are often confused and especially since, at the *Daedalus* conference of May 1963, a distinguished group of members reported their verdict that humanists are irresponsibly ignorant and neglectful of science.

To speak first of imaginative writers, if by ignorance is meant lack of technical competence in modern science, no doubt the charge is justified; but can it be wisely lodged at a time when the mathematician and the physicist, the biologist and the chemist are said to have imperfect understanding of one another? If, however, the charge means unawareness of the implications of science, its felt effects on life and thought and sensibility, it may be considered quite unjustified. One central impulse in modern American

[13] "An Evolutionist Looks at Modern Man," *Saturday Evening Post*, April 26, 1958, p. 122. I must add the stirring and disturbing paper by Dr. Eiseley, "The Illusion of the Two Cultures," *The American Scholar*, Summer 1964.

[14] *Daedalus*, Winter 1959, p. 141.

poetry and criticism has been opposition to the mechanizing and dehumanizing of man and insistence on his human individuality. Even current fiction — which, to speak with limited knowledge, may seem to have acquiesced too readily in the doctrine of the lost self — might defend its obsession with sex on similar grounds: man or woman, feeling dwarfed into nothingness by a big, mad, technological world, is moved in desperation to declare "*Amo* (or some less reputable word), *ergo sum.*" Such feelings may be exaggerated, but they cannot be dismissed as merely ignorant, stupid, or neurotic; in some degree they are quite common.

Shakespeare knew nothing of the up-to-date science of his day; he accepted as facts or as metaphors a multitude of things that were not so — and such ignorance did not matter in the least. If it is said that that may have been well enough long ago but will not do now, we might remember that Robert Frost, for instance, though perhaps not overburdened with intellectual knowledge, was well aware of science and was not crushed into surrender of individual human dignity with all its responsibilities and hazards. T. S. Eliot holds religious beliefs which most intellectuals regard as obsolete, but Mr. Eliot's poetry is a very significant part of our culture; he was indeed the first or one of the first of modern writers to discern some dominant characteristics of that culture, in particular the mechanization of the human spirit. I am not pleading for ignorance or in any way disparaging science (which would be imbecile); but it seems to me deplorable and disastrous when scientific thinkers assert that there is only one kind of knowledge, one kind of truth: that of verifiable experiment and analytical reason.[15] Nearly all science of the past

[15] E.g., Ernest Nagel: "These [poetry, painting, and music] are all im-

is now merely of historical interest; the literature of the past still speaks to us with a far more vital power than any scientific fact or idea commands. For a reminder of that obvious truth, this year 1964 is the four-hundredth anniversary of the birth of both Shakespeare and Galileo, but only one of the two is being celebrated everywhere (which is no reflection upon the greatness of Galileo).

As for the other community of humanists, the scholars, critics, and teachers, they certainly should know as much as they can absorb not only of modern science but of the whole history of science. No college teacher can deal with Donne or Milton or Pope or Shelley or Tennyson or many other poets, or with philosophers from Bacon onward, without dealing with science. In the last forty years or so literary scholarship has very fruitfully utilized — and even in many areas has written — the history of scientific ideas along with other ideas. And it is worth emphasizing that the many studies of science in relation to literature have come from literary scholars, mainly American, but not, so far as I recall, from scientists or historians of science; it seems to be assumed that the latter are either silent masters of literature or do not need to be. At any rate it is always the humanists who are charged with narrow ignorance; the charge gets its authority not from evidence but from repetition. We noted earlier the predominantly professional character of undergraduate courses in science, which are of small avail for humanistic laymen, though

portant and instructive forms of experience. But since nothing is stated by these objects in propositional form, in no intellegible sense can they be regarded as conveying truth or falsity. . . . In short, the contention that the humanities employ a distinctive conception of truth and represent a mode of knowledge different from scientific knowledge seems to me to be the consequence of a failure in analysis." *Daedalus*, Winter 1959, pp. 69–70. A layman might ask how one verifies the proposition that all truth is propositional — or is it simply a dogma?

scientists are given to blaming young humanists for not taking more of them. College courses in the humanities could be similarly professionalized, but it is in the spirit of the humanistic tradition to keep them broadly hospitable.

We all agree that the humanities, the natural sciences, and the social sciences are essential elements of a liberal education, though we might not agree about respective proportions. It has long been recognized, however, not merely that the three kinds of knowledge have grown further apart from one another, but that even the internal unity of these composite disciplines has given way to heterogeneous disunity, to the multiplication of splinter groups which may be almost as much divided from one another as the original three. We may deplore this state of affairs, though there seems to be no way of replacing the innumerable tribes of specialists with a new race of polymaths. It is also fairly obvious that, while such minute specialization has greatly speeded up the advance of knowledge on all fronts, it has impoverished the individual specialists, in the humanities no less than in the other areas. The full magnitude of the price we pay appears if we look around our world. As W. H. Auden remarked a while ago, anyone is considered crazy and almost immoral if he questions the unlimited desire for knowledge. Knowledge, we know, is power, and the long history of man, viewed on its darker side, is a history of struggles for power and profit, public or private; and that is sufficient ground for affirming that the exercise of moral wisdom, which includes imagination and taste, is a function of man as man — as a human being and not as a researcher. As individuals, many natural and social scientists may have a larger portion of moral wisdom than many humanists, but in this matter disparities in individual endowment are irrelevant. The point is that the natural and social sciences in themselves are morally detached and neutral — they pride themselves on being so — and are not directly concerned with the acquisition of moral wisdom. The intellectual symbol of our time is not man thinking and feeling but a computing machine.[16] The nonmoral nature of science is such that it can be and always has been used for both the benefit and the destruction of man; and in our age the destructive power has outdistanced everything else. One by-product of sociology's natural concern with averages and dominant patterns has been the translation, that is, the mistranslation — notably in pedagogical doctrine — of descriptive norms into positive ideals of uniformity and mediocrity.

Thus, as we have observed already, to many people it has appeared, with or without reason, that the sciences have tended to reduce individual man to a node or a statistical cipher, to make him feel a loss of identity. And, as we have also observed, it is in the creation of and response to literature and the arts (and in the ordinary personal relations of living) that human individuality — in the sense of total being, not merely intellect — is precious. Whatever the manifold deficiencies of humanists, the humanities in themselves are there to provide aesthetic, imaginative, and ethical experience; and the sum of individual experiences forms a large part of the more or less ordered pattern we live by, however shaken it is said to be in our time. The development of such experiences and such discipline is the whole reason for the existence of the humanities. (I am not speaking here of the

[16] Cf. P. LeCorbeiller: "Advances that have taken place in the last few years in the widely differing fields of automatic computation and of biochemistry will bring as vast a social revolution as did the steam engine, and they will have a greater philosophical impact than did evolution." *Daedalus*, Winter 1959, p. 174.

varied motives of creative artists but only of their audience.)

That is why it must be insisted that the humanities are the most basic of the three great bodies of knowledge and thought. I see no use in large vague pretences that the natural sciences, social sciences, and humanities are moving along convergent roads toward eventual unification. They are essentially different in origin, methods, and aims, and no spacious and specious generalities can gloss over the differences. In the old medical theory of the four humors, the body was healthy if the humors were in balance and unhealthy if one or other was present in excess. In our time the sickness of the cultural body has many causes, but one is surely the conspicuous excess of trust in the natural and social sciences as the sole or the main arteries of valuable truth and wisdom; and there seem to be few signs of any return to health. We may indeed reach a point in our new Dark Age — at moments one may wonder if we have not reached it already — where the literary creations of saner and nobler ages can no longer be assimilated or even dimly apprehended, where man has fulfilled his destiny as a mindless, heartless, will-less node. Meanwhile, no scientific problem is anywhere near so urgent as the preservation of individual man and his humane faculties and heritage.

I should like to end with utterances from three distinguished humanists, an architect, a scholar, and a poet. In a speech at Williams College Walter Gropius said:

> The vast development of science has thrown us out of balance. Science has overshadowed other components which are indispensable to the harmony of life. This balance must be reestablished. What we obviously need is a reorientation on the cultural level. . . . This is the century of science; the artist is only a luxury member of society. True art is doomed to languish as long as

science is supposed to have the only answers for our predominantly materialistic period.[17]

In a valedictory after his retirement from Harvard, Howard Mumford Jones, carrying on the Renaissance ideal of "virtue and good letters" and manfully opposing some fashionable clichés, affirmed that humane teaching must lead oncoming generations to ponder and accept "the changeless meaning of the three most powerful words in any dialect — justice, virtue, and love; concepts that arise out of history in spite of the fact that, or because, history too frequently denies them."[18] On the same occasion Archibald MacLeish, also retiring, said:

For only in literature — in the arts — in poetry — which contains the arts — only in poetry does *man* appear, man as he really is in his sordidness and his nobility. Elsewhere in the University man is a clinical specimen, or an intellectual abstraction, or a member of a mathematical equation, or a fixed point in a final dogma. Only with us is he himself — himself as Swift smelled him and as Keats saw him — himself in all his unimaginable — unimaginable if literature had not perceived them — possibilities.[19]

[17] *New York Times*, September 23, 1963.
[18] *Harvard Alumni Bulletin*, LXV (1963), 309.
[19] Ibid., p. 310.

Literary History and Literary Criticism

I CONFESS THAT every time I have looked through the program for this Congress I have been stricken with inarticulate paralysis. Almost every topic is a reminder of the infinite extent of literature and criticism and of one's own infinite ignorance. While there may be polymaths among us who have no reason to be so troubled, it can probably be assumed that most scholars and critics have some acquaintance with despair, unless they early reconciled themselves to picking up pebbles on the shore or cultivating their own small garden.

The scope of the program and one's individual sense of total inadequacy in some sense dramatize a general problem which nowadays confronts not merely literary humanists but workers in all areas of intellectual endeavor. There is just too much to know, not only of literature itself and the vast amount of scholarship and criticism but of cultural history in general, since the study of literature takes in everything that man has felt and thought and done, including science and the arts. Up through the nineteenth

Reprinted by permission from *Literary History and Literary Criticism: Acta of the Ninth Congress International Federation for Modern Languages and Literature Held at New York University, August 25 to 31, 1963*, ed. Leon Edel, K. McKee, and W. M. Gibson (New York: New York University Press, 1965).

century "literature" as a matter of course meant only or chiefly European literature; now the conventional boundaries have been widely extended, and both the more and the less familiar bodies of writing have been studied in breadth and depth by relatively new armies of professional scholars and critics. The contrast between the literary scene in 1963 and that of 1863 does not need elaboration, although it is so significant in various ways that I shall be coming back to it.

These self-evident considerations — and again the list of topics and of foreign experts in our program — are good warrant for caution, and I shall stay discreetly within the limits of scholarship and criticism in the English-speaking world. Whether attitudes and movements in this restricted area are parallel to, or quite different from, those found in continental Europe and elsewhere, they are important in themselves and complex enough for a brief survey.

We might recall some tendencies and landmarks in the England and America of the last hundred years and especially the last fifty or so. In England, for a good part of that period it was assumed that one read one's native literature for oneself, without academic instruction. While academic scholarship of the modern kind was being produced, in the outer world criticism was mainly impressionistic "appreciation." The critical work of the early 1900's that proved to be of most enduring importance was A. C. Bradley's *Shakespearean Tragedy*, the culminating product of the nineteenth-century romantic tradition; in literary history a large landmark was Courthope's philosophic *History of English Poetry*. But if we had to name the single figure most typical of English criticism and literary history in that period, it would be George Saintsbury, the amateur *par excellence*, the quite unphilosophical embodiment of omnivorous gusto. Saintsbury's history of English literature and his larger history of criticism surveyed countless individual writers with only minimal recognition of the movement of ideas, of critical and cultural processes and patterns. While France and Italy also had their traditions of impressionism, we may think of the semi-scientific principles of Taine or of the philosophical De Sanctis. During the last forty years professionalism in England has grown much stronger, though there are still a good many books written for, and sometimes apparently by, the general reader (not that that is such a bad thing, since it implies a popular audience).

In the nineteenth century the United States had its amateurs, like Poe — whose impact on France was so significant — and James Russell Lowell. There was also such a scholarly historian of American literature as Moses Coit Tyler. But we may associate the general rise of American literary scholarship with the establishment and growth of graduate schools in the major universities. In this country the professional attitude has been much more firmly fixed than the amateur; one conspicuous early achievement was Child's great edition of the popular ballads. To speak roughly, from about 1880 to about 1916 there was virtually a single movement in literary scholarship, that is, the writing of literary history according to the genetic method, a method derived from European science and the literary stress on milieu. This meant the tracing of literary sources and literary influences, and during most of this long period the material was predominantly medieval literature, which lent itself most readily to such investigations and which had such illustrious European explorers as Gaston Paris. The aim and method, however, were extended over later literature as well, and continued to flourish through the 1930's, after rival aims and methods had appeared. The total result, whether in rounded works or small fragments, was a learned, comprehensive, and solidly detailed body of literary history from which we have all learned. Its chief shortcoming was that its historical preoccupations slighted criticism and critical values, so that it remained largely an external record of purely literary relationships. One book which may be called at once a culmination and a distinguished exception was John Livingston Lowes's *The Road to Xanadu* (1927).

While this useful if limited approach to literature is still practiced to some degree (and in recent years has been rehabilitated by a more critical historicism), it gave way to a succession of movements which sought to get closer to the inner significance and artistic value of literature. The second great wave in the United States was the history of ideas. Irving Babbitt, the Harvard professor of French, had been a crusader, on his own ethical and anti-Romantic plane. More disinterested modes of inquiry seem to have begun about 1916 on several literary fronts, in the writings of a number of literary scholars and of the philosopher Arthur O. Lovejoy. This new movement, in part a revolt against the tyranny of external fact, had a strong appeal for those, especially the young, who craved more nourishment from literature than literary history had provided. For many years many notable scholars have been rewriting the history of literature — and not merely of literature — with a fresh understanding of the complex pressures of religious, philosophical, scientific, ethical, social, political, and aesthetic ideas. There is no need of citing authors of the many books and articles, American and English, which are part of everyone's equipment. The study of ideas has not only re-created literary history at a new depth; it has come closer to criticism through its philosophical illumination of countless individual works and authors.

But neither the older literary history nor the history of ideas carried within itself any criteria of aesthetic values, since a poor writer might illustrate influences or ideas as well as, or even better than, a great one. Also, both methods were focused primarily on backgrounds or specific strains in literature and did not essay fully rounded accounts of particular works. To fill this partial vacuum the so-called "new criticism" came into being; the name, in America, arrived some time after the method had been in full swing. The close analysis of rhetorical structure and texture had been employed with the classics ever since antiquity, but classical education had long been declining and with it the capacity for intensive reading. To recall some familiar facts, the modern revival or adaptation of rhetorical analysis began with the general stimulus of the anti-Romantic T. E. Hulme and T. S. Eliot and the more rigorous principles and practice of I. A. Richards and his disciples, such as William Empson. Although the new criticism started in England, it spread widely and rapidly in the United States, so that before long no department of English could count itself respectable unless it included at least one new critic. The virtues and the limitations of the new criticism everyone knows. Although literary history and the history of ideas are valuable disciplines in themselves, it is individual works that stir us, and the new criticism focused directly on them. It taught slack generations to read, to analyze the functional components of works of art, form, imagery, diction, rhythm, and such qualities as irony, ambiguity, and paradox. It also tended, if not consistently, to take works out of their historical setting; and it could emphasize some elements, such as imagery, at the expense of others and thereby fall into overreading or misreading. Speaking recently of such dangers, Professor M. H. Abrams judiciously affirmed that "The necessary but not sufficient condition for a competent reader of poetry remains what it has always been — a keen eye for the obvious."[1] In general the new criticism has had more success with short poems of an intellectual cast than with other things from pure lyrics to epics, plays, and novels.

Some other approaches to literature may be mentioned more briefly. They range from a mainly social view (which in the 1930's could be dogmatic Marxism) to the aims and scientific methods of technical bibliography. Apropos of the latter, it might be observed that of late years scholarly acumen and rigor have been assisted by time-saving machines for the collating of texts and the like — a new and startling version of the wedding of Mercury and Philology. Another and less scientific approach — though it can claim scientific origins and authority — has come from the psychology of Freud and others. This has often inclined to loose or extreme exploitation of over-simple formulas; it has also, as in some large works by French scholar-critics, utilized psychology in more general and flexible ways. Then there is the neo-Aristotelian school, centered in the University of Chicago, which has put critical emphasis on structure; and there are other forms of formalism. There are the structural linguists, who have quickly become a considerable army, but whose work I am not qualified to assess. Some scholars, trained in the old way as literary historians, have brought literary and other kinds of learning to the theory and practice of criticism. And a number of

[1] "Five Ways of Reading *Lycidas*," *Varieties of Literary Experience*, ed. Stanley Burnshaw (New York, 1962), p. 23.

important scholars and critics cannot be readily classified. To add a last topic to this overcrowded paragraph, from the new critics onward there has been an inclination to deny biography a place in or near criticism, but, for one recent and distinguished interpretative work, there are the volumes on Henry James by the local chairman of this Congress, Professor Leon Edel. Among other new works that fuse biography and criticism are two by younger colleagues of mine, Herschel Baker's *William Hazlitt* and W. J. Bate's *John Keats*.

In this country perhaps the most fashionable critical mode of the past decade or more has been the myth-and-symbol doctrine. Like the new criticism, it began in England but has flourished chiefly in America. It may be said to have started with Maud Bodkin's *Archetypal Patterns in Poetry* (1934); its authoritative bible is the fresh, acute, learned, and lively *Anatomy of Criticism* (1957) by Northrop Frye. This doctrine has grown out of psychology and anthropology, especially the writings of Jung, out of such seminal works of modern literature as *The Waste Land* and *Ulysses*, and in some sense out of the new criticism, although that father does not care to acknowledge any parenthood. In capable hands, this method has added new dimensions to many works of literature or has firmly defined dimensions and traditional patterns felt only vaguely before. In less capable hands it can yield quite erratic fancies, since the wandering eye sees myths and symbols everywhere, and some products are paralleled only by the medieval religious allegorizations of Ovid. Even at its best this method, having such a special focus, can hardly render a full account of any particular work. Its most general limitation is that, like the old literary history and the history of ideas, it does not contain in itself any criteria of aesthetic value; of course, like literary historians and historians of ideas, myth-and-symbol critics may acquire such criteria from elsewhere and use them.

To return to literary history, which includes both formal histories of periods and genres and innumerable particular contributions, we have noticed the two main kinds, the strictly literary and the ideological. Most of the formal histories of English literature, large and small, are mainly literary, although the largest, the *Cambridge History*, cast its net over wide areas. I take it that in the theme of our program "literary history" means both kinds. But there have been and are diverse opinions about the proper scope of histories of literature — and a few strong-minded individualists object to their being written at all. Some people would confine history to works of conscious art and to the historical charting of these in aesthetic terms. Others would argue that the serious botanist is not content with flowers in a bouquet but wants to examine root, branches, leaves, and even soil, the whole organism in its habitat. In other words, literary history can be conceived as the record not only of works of art but of all forms of culture expressed in the written word. Both kinds of course must be critical and in some sense philosophical. I think that there is room and need for both kinds, although I favor the broader conception. Literary history devoted wholly to aesthetic concerns is likely to be "too thin breathing," as Keats's Endymion said of his direct pursuit of an abstract ideal; it is a diet for epicures and needs some roughage. The broader kind of history does much to re-create the mental worlds of the authors it deals with; and it makes a much stronger appeal to the general reader, if he still exists or can be brought back into existence. In this connection I might say that it seems to me deplorable that the one consecutive survey of

English literature in popular form should be the Pelican volumes edited by Boris Ford and written by the heirs of *Scrutiny*; there are good sections, but not enough to redeem the whole.

To sum up the accomplishment of our own century, it can be safely said that an immense amount of varied learning and infinite rays of philosophical and critical light have been brought to bear on the whole range of English and American literature, that we now have — or groups of specialists now have — vastly richer knowledge and understanding than anyone possessed or dreamed of in the later nineteenth century. The whole scale and aim and method of study have gone well beyond what was for centuries considered appropriate for the ancient classics only. In 1888 Arnold could say that "Shelley is not a classic, whose various readings are to be noted with earnest attention"; now, of course, Shelley and all the other major and many minor poets are edited with meticulous textual apparatus. Most of us could not, without hesitation, recall the chief scholarly and critical books that were around 1890 available for students of English and American literature; now there are whole libraries. During this period professional journals have multiplied to a number that makes the head swim. In the annual international bibliography in *PMLA* the list of books and articles on English and American literature runs, in recent years, to more than six thousand.

This has been, I hope, a fair if meager outline of the American and English scene. Obviously the catholic impressionist orthodoxy of the age of Saintsbury has given place to a variety of protestant creeds and sects, not all in harmony with one another and some claiming an exclusive hold upon truth. Obviously also, no one person could or would be a practicing adherent of all the diverse creeds and methods. We all do what we best can and like to do. But, since the map presents a confusing number of roads, divergent, parallel, or convergent, we may well ask not merely where we go from here but where we are now. I cannot answer either question, but I shall venture to make some comments; I shall probably not escape the dangers both of seeming to pontificate and of being much too elementary for this very learned and sophisticated audience.

1. The name of Arnold recalls his broad definition of criticism, which made no specific reference to literature at all and was indeed virtually the same as his definition of culture. In our time criticism in that large sense is carried on, by philosophic publicists and others, but criticism in the narrower sense, as we have seen, has been moving along very diverse roads, most of them leading to partial rather than total views of a work or an author. Ideally, criticism seeks to define and analyze both the substantive materials and the aesthetic components of a particular work, both being considered as the means of expressing a theme; it seeks also to interpret that theme and to assess the total value of the work in itself and in relation to comparable works. The terms of this rough definition need to be enlarged though not essentially altered if the critic is dealing with more than one work or with an author's whole output. Along with the critic's own quest of light and satisfaction, his main object is to mediate between a work or author and a reader presumably less instructed and enlightened, at least on this particular topic. As Mr. Eliot succinctly put it, the function of criticism is the elucidation of works of art and the correction of taste; and, as he also said, comparison and analysis are the critic's chief instruments.

2. Since the great mass of great literature belongs to the

past, adequate criticism must grow out of historical knowledge, cultural and linguistic, as well as out of intuitive insight. Every work must be understood on its own terms as the product of a particular mind in a particular setting, and that mind and setting must be re-created through all the resources that learning and the historical imagination can muster — not excluding the author's intention, if that is known. The very pastness of a work, as Lionel Trilling [2] has emphasized, is part of its meaning for us and must be realized to the best of our power. The doctrine that a work of art is self-sufficient and may not receive extraneous illustration is arbitrary and irrational. There are no short cuts to the past or present significance of a work of the past, though uninformed criticism has the advantage that Sir Robert Walpole found in having bawdy conversation at the dinner table — that all could join in on equal terms. We can of course achieve only limited degrees of truth in trying to re-create the outward and inward conditions in which a work of art was engendered, but, unless we try, we cannot distinguish between its local and temporal and its universal and timeless elements; indeed we may not be able to understand some works at all.

One example of unhistorical distortion is the way in which, during the 1920's and later, John Donne was turned into a skeptical, rootless, alienated, twentieth-century intellectual. Or we might take such an example of wrongheadedness as the book on *Paradise Lost* by A. J. A. Waldock, who belabored the poem because its characters and narrative were not those of a realistic novel and who, in regard to religious and even ethical values, was simply tone deaf. Thomas Rymers, when they appear, suffer from lack of knowledge or lack of imagination or both. One function

[2] "The Sense of the Past," *The Liberal Imagination* (New York, 1950).

of literary history is to correct the vagaries of unhistorical criticism. History and criticism were taken as one and indivisible by Edmund Wilson (who is probably tired of being called the dean of American critics): in dedicating *Axel's Castle* (1931) to his Princeton teacher, Christian Gauss, Mr. Wilson said that it was principally from him that he acquired his idea of what literary criticism ought to be, "a history of man's ideas and imaginings in the setting of the conditions which have shaped them."

3. While criticism cannot attain to anything like scientific objectivity, it should seek to avoid personal bias. Mr. Eliot long ago quoted the saying of Rémy de Gourmont, that every critic, if he is sincere, tries to erect his personal impressions into laws. In that sense, the great lawgiver of our time is F. R. Leavis. A critic cannot escape his own temperamental and intellectual limitations, and should not deny his own convictions and standards, but he should be open-mindedly receptive to works of art and the critical ideas of others. This might seem a truism if there were not critics who appear otherwise disposed. The various kinds of criticism already outlined can be the means of illumination; they can also be idols of the cave. What are we to say when a learned and often acute critic of *Paradise Lost* finds in the poem phallicism, castration complexes, and other elements of the rigmarole? Miltonic criticism yields an especially rich harvest of prejudice and aberration. While Mr. Eliot's poetry has long been classical and in no need of defense, it has long been recognized that his early criticism was in part an oblique justification of his own poetic methods, among them the use of concrete particulars. Mr. Eliot could apply this principle to *L'Allegro* without regard to Milton's purpose: the ploughman and the rest were not made individuals, as Wordsworth would have seen them. But Milton

needed typical, ideal figures in a landscape, and the effect would have been ruined if he had told us that the ploughman, like Wordsworth's Simon Lee, had weak ankles that swelled. Similarly Dr. Leavis denounced Milton's description of paradise because it did not give the immediate sensation of being in a garden; here again, in a symbolic pattern of perfection in which the garden and its inhabitants must be kept at an aesthetic distance, realistic particularity would have been fatal.

4. Since criticism is not a science and cannot be made one by any amount of theorizing, it should follow the world's great critics in the belief that the most precise and subtle ideas about literature can be expressed in ordinary language. Some English exponents of "Cambridge English" and some Americans are given to horrid pseudo-scientific diction embedded in shapeless, jagged, cacophonous sentences. Jargon does not make simple ideas scientific and profound; it only inspires profound distrust of the user's aesthetic sensitivity. I might mention a sinister declaration I had from a sophomore who came in to tell me that he was a Thomist in his thinking and also to speak about his low marks. I asked "Did you ever in all your reading encounter such clotted jargon as this paper?" Said he, "I write the English of the future."

5. Of literature, especially poetry, in the modern languages a very large part is bound up with the classics, and it may be thought that modern criticism suffers from the general decline of classical education. Such education, to be sure, is no guarantee of insight, but it is likely to promote centrality and rationality of outlook and clarity of style and to be an asset worth more than methodologies.

6. A sixth generality, which belongs to the other end of the spectrum, can also be put briefly. Academic scholars

and critics nowadays are as a rule much more aware of contemporary writing than they used to be, much more aware that literature is not something that stopped decades ago and was enshrined in a museum, but something that goes on, continually augmented by people who live among us. And there is much more osmosis than there was between the academy and the outer world of writers. Such awareness of the present is good in itself and it helps to vitalize our sense of the past.

7. My last comment requires some elaboration. During the twenty-five centuries from Homer to about 1800, the long stretch of time that brought forth a very high proportion of the world's great literature, there was only a trickle of what can be termed specific criticism; and literary history, though called for by Bacon, did not appear in England until the eighteenth century. It would seem that literature can thrive without either, and that perhaps we have no good reason for existing. I would not deny for a moment the splendid achievements of modern scholarship and criticism, which were briefly celebrated earlier, and to which we are all grateful debtors; but the picture has its other side and candor compels a look at that.

With all our solid grounds for satisfaction, even complacency, there are grounds also for depression, though I do not know whether this is widespread; possibly foreign scholars and critics feel it less, or less directly, than many of us in the United States, which has by far the largest army of workers in the vineyard and produces by far the largest quantity of grapes, juicy or dry. Of course there are practical and professional pressures that explain some of this activity. But whatever the writers' motives, from the desire for promotion to the sharing of a fresh insight, it is an obvious fact that no one, even if he had nothing to do but read, could assimilate more than a fraction of the material that deals with his own special interests, much less anything beyond these. No one can pick his way through a few sections of one of the annual bibliographies before another huge volume has fallen upon him. A footnote is blown up into an article, an article into a book. Again and again, reading articles and books that in large measure say what has been said many times before, we ask the question asked under wartime restrictions: "Was this trip necessary?" Some critical analyses seem designed to supersede and bury the original work. Criticism has become less of an art than a grim industry or solemn priestcraft, and in the process has lost most of the infectious gusto that used to inspire amateur impressionism in less doggedly conscientious times. In short, the great achievements of scholarship and criticism have their pathological side, and we seem to have encountered the law of diminishing returns. Then, to look outside our immediate professional concerns, when and how do we enlarge our acquaintance with the infinite body of the world's great literature and the extra-literary works that we should know? But one recoils from considering the answer to that question.

In the present state of the cultural and the political world I do not think that we can afford to continue our recent course without taking more thought about where we stand and where we are going. I can only ask forgiveness if I end with gratuitous sermonizing, though I imagine that I am expressing a general uneasiness. We students of literature assembled here, representing many countries with more or less venerable literary traditions, may have for the moment a feeling of confident strength and security. But that feeling, if we have it, is surely something of an illusion. Without repeating the clichés about possible annihilation, we must still recognize the fact that, after some two millennia of leadership, the humanities have in our time been downgraded by the dazzling discoveries of science and, to a lesser degree, by the large promises of social science. The past twenty or thirty years have witnessed the birth of a new scientific civilization. We and other tribes of humanists — and some scientists — deny the multiplying and aggressive claims of the sciences that they are the supreme or the only guides for mankind, we maintain that the humanities are still the realm of value and the central habitation of the human spirit, but we are engaged in what has the appearance of a losing battle. Possibly, if he survives, man will discover that he cannot live, literally or metaphorically, in the mechanized and dehumanized world of science and technology, and the Zeitgeist will alter its present course. But we cannot put our faith in that dubious deity; perhaps we cannot do much of anything. Yet we can surely do something better than go our accustomed ways without regard to the advent of a new dark age.

In the study of literature as in the sciences modern specialization has of course added enormously and rapidly to the total sum of knowledge and enlightenment, but the individual specialists, if not reduced to the humble function of coral insects, have at any rate been impoverished. The serious humanists of the Renaissance were intellectual and cultural, ethical and political leaders of their world. A century ago the Sainte-Beuves and Arnolds could address a large public with authority and be heard. How many literary humanists nowadays have any semblance of that general authority? Such men as Sainte-Beuve and Arnold were amateurs in a number of literatures; most of us are experts in patches of one. It is not our fault that a once considerable and fairly homogeneous public has almost if not quite disappeared, yet we have done more to assist than to check the process. We seldom think of addressing any but an academic audience, old or young; we write for other scholars and critics on relatively esoteric matters and seldom try, in Arnoldian language, to enlarge the saving remnant. There was, to be sure, indifference or hostility toward the humanities in ancient Athens and Renaissance Europe, but now the adverse odds are immensely heavier. We ourselves, in our libraries or in the company of colleagues, are so sure of our own faith in literature that we forget how minute a portion of the human race we are, how alien and meaningless that faith is to most of mankind, how greatly the world has changed from the relative security and traditionalism of the nineteenth century. I do not mean that we should forsake true learning for the pulpit (as I am now doing in addressing a body of the elect), that we should go about giving inspirational hurrahs for the humanities — though even such utterances can be desirable at times. But I do believe that we should turn a much larger part of our energies to sharing our central faith, that we should not allow ourselves to be drawn away from the essential values of literature, that we should put much less effort into the indiscriminate advancement of knowledge. As I said at the start, there is already far too much to know, in literature itself, without taking account of scholarship and criticism at all. We are in a perpetual rat race, neglecting original works because we must keep up with new knowledge and opinions. Perhaps, as I remarked before, these baneful pressures are worse in this country than elsewhere — I do not know. But foreign scholars may still agree that the study of literature, with all its visible and splendid accomplishment, could be in a much healthier state, that it could reflect much more truly and fully our highest faith and aims. If we cannot any longer achieve or deserve the status of the early humanists, we can at least strive not to dwindle into a society of antiquaries and connoisseurs "Housed in a dream, at distance from the kind."